Christ is in you!

By the same author:

Esoteric Christianity – A Tragic History
The Way of Wisdom – The Art of Meditation
Poems for the Path
Patrick and the Holy Grail
Gnosis!

SEAN BYRNE

Christ is in you!

THE ESSENCE OF ESOTERIC CHRISTIANITY

AGE-OLD
BOOKS

Published by AGE-OLD BOOKS in N. Ireland

Copyright © Sean Byrne 2014

Contact: ageoldbooksinfo@gmail.com

ISBN: 978-0-9540255-8-8

A catalogue record of this book is available from the British Library.

AGE-OLD
BOOKS

Contents

Keep the secret sense celestial
Of the starry birth;
Though about you call the bestial
Voices of the earth.

George Russell (AE)

INTRODUCTION

When Christianity first began in the Roman Empire 2000 years ago, it was an esoteric sect. Christians were a small group who believed in a new and very strange god, so strange he had to be worshipped in secret, underground.

Vilified, hated and persecuted initially, the Christians nevertheless grew in number and became an unstoppable force. In time they were not only tolerated and accepted, but actually gave birth to a whole new worldview and social order, organised from Rome, in fact a whole new civilization, so that nowadays Christianity is not esoteric anymore.

Or is it?

Surely the question we must ask is: what precisely did these first 'esoteric Christians' believe? How precisely did they regard their strange new god?

It is, of course, a difficult question to answer, given the timescale involved. One thing is certain, however: the truly enlightening spirit Being, the God who once lived and thrived at the centre of the movement he gave rise to, the Church, has become little more than a hollow shell. The beautiful white pearl of the Christ, the 'Living Stone' which constituted early Christianity's 'esoteric' foundation, and which was set so lovingly into the hearts of his most faithful followers, is lost or forgotten. Christ nowadays is just another word, another name, another god among the many.

In truth, however, this name and this God is unique. And this book will tell you why.

We can begin by taking the shell in which the Christ spirit once lived, putting it to our ears and listening carefully. Then we will surely hear echoes of the past, names and voices that can still inspire. Mainstream Christianity cannot do this. The modern Church provides little nourishment for the soul. And never has the soul needed nourishment more than today. Never have we hungered more deeply for the 'Bread of Life'. But to find it these dark days we must listen very carefully, and search very hard; we must, in fact, go on a long journey, a pilgrimage.

With this book, dear reader, you can begin this journey. It is a journey of discovery and rediscovery, of recovery and of self-learning. Here begins your search for sounds, signs and symbols, for words that will guide you to a place where that pearl of purest knowledge, that solid rock of faith so firmly possessed by the early 'esoteric' followers of the Christ, can become yours, and so powerfully alive in your soul that it will awaken your vision, enrich your mind, invigorate your heart and heal your wounds.

CHAPTER 1

THE COSMIC CHRIST

The very early believers or followers of Christ Jesus can also be called gnostic Christians. Gnosis is Greek for knowledge, so the term indicates that they really knew the Christ. These men and women were often, though by no means always, Jews, but not the kind of Jews that Jesus continually rails against in the Gospels, i.e. the Pharisees, the Sadducees, the Scribes etc., whose only concern was for the letter of the Law and who cared little for its spirit.

This early gnostic Church attracted people from very varied backgrounds. Many of them were familiar with the Hebrew Mysteries and some were even initiates thereof. Others came from the Greek religions where Adonis or Bacchus was worshipped, or from the Persian Mysteries of Mithras which were widely practised at this time. Because of this, the vast Oriental wisdom played a prominent part in shaping and directing the spiritual dynamics of the early Christian movement.

Whereas the Jews saw in Jesus little more than a mad prophet who deserved to die for blaspheming against their Law, the gnostic Christians saw in him the incarnation of an Avatar, one of those godlike beings of the Oriental religions who from time to time walked the Earth.

Whether orally or in written form, these early gnostic followers of the Christ were familiar with that magnificent wisdom-tradition of the East which long predates Christianity and is known as the Upanishads. The pearl at the heart of these ancient teachings, the fantastic discovery made over and over again by the sages who compiled and recorded them, is that the source of all manifestation, the origin of all being, knowledge and truth, is the Self. In other words, they equated the Self with God.

The cultivation of self-knowledge was at the heart of *all* the ancient Mysteries. 'Know yourself, and you will know both the Universe and the Gods' was the inscription writ large over the door of the Temple of Delphi. That the same knowledge was also cultivated in the Hebrew Mysteries is apparent from a famous scene in the biblical Book of Genesis in which Moses comes upon the Burning Bush. Here a god appears to him in Promethean fashion, as a mighty flame. This god beckons Moses, and he hears him in clearly audible words. Moses is greatly perplexed. He felt that he knew God very well. Had his God not delivered him and his people out of slavery in Egypt? Moses's God had spoken to him often out of the depths of his soul, but he had never encountered him as a physically visible and speaking flame before. So, as he listens and stares with great awe and wonder at this Burning Bush, Moses becomes fearful that it might be a manifestation of some repugnant foreign god, one of those old deities who were forever trying to seduce his people away from the One True God, the One whom Moses, and the Hebrew initiates generally, knew to be fundamentally different from all the others. So, plucking up a mighty courage, Moses impertinently asks this flaming entity its name, and receives the astounding reply: '*I Am* is my name' (Exodus, 3:14).

This is the clearest possible indication that the ancient, Eastern self-knowledge was also at the heart of the Hebrew Mysteries. That it was also cultivated in early Christianity, which was strongly influenced by the Hebrew religion, can easily be deduced from John's 'esoteric' Gospel, where, using archetypal imagery, Jesus refers to himself seven times as the fulfilment, the embodiment, nay the living incarnation of the ancients', but most especially the Hebrews', 'I Am' God. In various places in John's Gospel, but in the following sequence, Jesus says: '*I am* the Bread of Life'; '*I am* the Light of the World'; '*I am* the Door'; '*I am* the Good Shepherd'; '*I am* the Resurrection and the Life'; '*I am* the Way, the Truth and the Life'; '*I am* the True Vine'.

We will have much more to say throughout this book about these profound *I Am* sayings of John's Jesus, and their wonderful capacity to stir and strengthen the imagination, to educate and nourish the soul of the true seeker of spiritual knowledge, which in our time must be esoteric, for in order to really *know* Christ, we must get back to the roots of his Christianity. In order to discover or rediscover this esoteric content of Christianity, we must, in a sense, travel back in time, excavate spiritually, roll up our spiritual sleeves, as it were, and do some hard, inner work, for we will have to clear away centuries of dogmatic debris that has accumulated like a hard shell around a once living, loving and vibrant reality, the human-divine, *I Am* Being, about whom John writes with such intimate and spiritually revealing knowledge.

Excavating thus, we will get to the esoteric, core truths of Jesus the Christ, and out of this knowledge establish a living, loving and faithful relationship with this Master of all masters, and become just like one of his first followers.

***

We live in an abominable spiritual wilderness regarding the truth of Christ Jesus. His vibrantly living Word has been imprisoned in stone churches, cold cathedrals, canon laws, obscure dogmas or dusty old books. The Church, that body whose original function was to spread Christ's living Word, has completely lost its way. Nowadays it has become little more than a matrix of sects, infighting over the meaning of their various doctrines and dogmas. But there are no dogmas in Esoteric Christianity. Dogmas were tools evolved by a now obsolete 'Age of Faith' in which so-called Christianity was forced by tired and ruined Rome down the necks of the virile young tribes of Europe. The main idea was to curb their passion, soften their manners and haul them into some kind of civilized life as the Romans themselves had long understood and cultivated it. Nowadays, however, we live in a new and freer age, an 'age of knowledge', or science. It is not sufficient to simply *believe* anymore; we need to *know*.

Not that faith is unimportant. It still is. Nowadays, however, it must be supplemented with knowledge. We positively thirst as a species now for a true knowledge of the spirit, even a *science* of the spirit. Dead dogmas and outdated doctrines cannot provide a moral basis for acquiring this knowledge. Quite the reverse. They act merely as walls, as barriers, as 'limitations of knowledge'. The early 'esoteric' Christians had a powerful love of and faith in the Christ because they cultivated *knowledge* of him. This knowledge can return to the modern seeker, but only through what we have to call Esoteric Christianity.

By consciously deciding to take up Esoteric Christianity you embark on a journey, the most important journey you are ever likely to make: the magical, mystical journey of *gnosis*. This is a journey that leads to knowledge of your true self, which is born of the Self of the world. Christ Jesus is your 'Light on the Path'. He said: 'I am the Light of the world' (John, 8:12).

Before we begin that journey, however, we must establish a few fundamentals to orientate us.

Esoteric Christianity differs in many significant respects from mainstream, or what we may call orthodox, Christianity. Perhaps the chief of these differences is that Esoteric Christianity calls attention to, and elaborates with profound knowledge, the Cosmic Christ. Orthodox Christianity, by contrast, asserts merely that Christ Jesus was both a god and a human being. If one questions the divine nature of Jesus, however, one is met only with a confused muddle of thoughts.

In the early Gnostic Church there was no such muddle. Whatever about the general mass of Jesus's followers at that time, the enlightened ones certainly knew how to regard Jesus. They knew, for instance, that Jesus was simply his *human* name. But the deeper secret was contained in the fact that Christ was his divine name. They knew, in fact, that this truth was the precise key to understanding the human/divine nature of the long prophesied Jewish Messiah, the Anointed One of the Hebrew Mysteries. The enlightened regarded Jesus himself as the fulfilment of these Mysteries, as the Letter to the Hebrews in the New Testament clearly shows.

Thus, a rich gnosis was cultivated in early Christianity. A fuller meaning of the word "gnosis" would be something like 'knowledge of the ancient Mysteries', and it is therefore correct to speak of the early Christian movement, up to about the first half of the 3rd century, as the Gnostic Church. (The word "Church" to these first Christians meant simply the Risen Body of the Lord.) From its very inception, however, this movement was hated not only by the Jewish establishment, but more importantly, by imperial Rome itself. Even long before Christianity emerged, the emperors detested the secrecy of the Mysteries. They wanted to be gods themselves, and everywhere they went they bribed, cajoled and corrupted the local priesthood, vitiating their spiritual power. Many of the emperors were driven mad by a demonic desire for absolute, divine power.

Thus, when Christianity became a force, they aimed their hatred at the Gnostics. But Christianity was an unstoppable force, and not just spiritually, but socially and culturally also, so that eventually the Romans had no choice but to embrace it. Although traditional mainstream

Christianity presents this as the best thing that ever happened to the Church, it was in fact the absolute worst. For the Romans embraced Christianity merely because they saw in it a movement that could be manipulated for political, monetary and military advantage. Their embrace was in fact the kiss of death for true Christianity.

It is actually very difficult to imagine just how much Rome hated the Gnostics. After a long battle they eventually got rid of them, and then, with their foot firmly in the door of Christianity, began to mould its God in their own imperial image, an image based on ignorance, superstition and absolute hatred of the ancient Mysteries. They dragged the image of God, as newly revealed through the incarnated Christ, down to the level of one of their half-mad emperors and made a purely earthly image of him out of Jesus the man. They suppressed, in other words, all talk of the Cosmic Christ, outlawed all true spiritual knowledge of him, and in this way the key to the ancient mystery of God and the heavenly origin of his Anointed One was thrown away and lost for a very long time to come.

From about the 4th century onward, beginning with the conniving of that most bellicose of all the late emperors, Constantine, true spiritual knowledge was forced out of the Christian movement, and the earthly or the purely human aspect of the great new Godman, the Jesus aspect only, was promulgated. This was due fundamentally to the mentality of Rome. They firmly fixed the agenda for the Christian movement for the next one and a half thousand years by making the Bishop of Rome take over the Pontiff Maximus title of the defunct emperors. He then became Pope and ruler of a great, new, but very unspiritual world religion. Somehow this monstrosity – the only possible word for a religion without spirit - held together up to the Reformation, but it was shaken to its very foundations during the Enlightenment. The 20th century saw an end to it, and for this we can surely be thankful.

There are similarities between our own time (in the West) and the early Gnostic Church. Conventional religion was as dead as doornails when Jesus was born, as it is now. It was John the Baptist who in this wilderness cried out to his people to awaken to the inevitability that they would lose all contact with the spiritual world if they did not change their ways. After Jesus was baptized by John, he took over this call. Jesus was, in fact, known to the Gnostics as 'The Awakener'.

This call is made again today by modern Esoteric Christianity. The mainstream Church today is a kind of decrepit zombie in our midst, an embarrassment to all true Christians, a thing quite incapable of renewal or genuine reformation, whether from within or without. It is spiritual corpse. But true Christians know, and have always known down the dark, forbidding centuries, that the Christ will never die, *cannot* ever die. He is very much alive! But he is no longer interested in either promoting or sustaining a dark, death-worshipping faith. Whatever the purpose of all that horror was, it has been served. Its day is done. Faith nowadays, if it is to be real, meaningful and strong, must be imbued with a new light, the light of a living ethereal Being who, as many are aware, is drawing ever closer to our world. This is the One we call the Cosmic Christ. His reappearance has long been prophesied and it is a reality happening now. However, we can only *understand* it through Esoteric Christianity.

CHAPTER 2

THE BANISHMENT AND RETURN OF SOPHIA

We will return in Chapter 11 to the most important spiritual phenomenon of our time, the Second Coming or the reappearance of the Christ. To get to grips with this phenomenon, however, we must first turn to a spiritual Being with whom, as part of the Godhead, Christ is intimately associated. This is Sophia.

Despite what many of us were taught as children, God does not have a big, long, white beard. Indeed, he is not a man at all - or if he is, he is as much a woman as a man. In fact, in this regard the male Jesus babe at the breast of the Madonna is as good an image of God as any. It was indeed the Church's traditional way of representing its God, i.e. the incarnated Christ, to its flock, and there was a certain wisdom in it. It was, alas, a wisdom that the Church from very early on in its history sacrificed to a blind and dark faith, for it banned all possibility of *understanding* the Incarnation.

Understanding is another term for wisdom. It is female and intuitive in character, the opposite of the analytical male mind which characteristically produces sharp, cut-and-dried definitions, dogmas and formulae. Tragically, this female or wisdom side of the Incarnation, so enthusiastically cultivated by the Gnostics, was systematically erased from Christianity by the Roman patriarchy. Very early on, the latter began replacing a philosophical approach to the Christ with a narrow, dogmatic theology that placed strict limitations on human knowledge, thereby imprisoning the natural wisdom of the soul. It was an agenda born of ignorance, and hatred of the feminine, and a strategy simply asking for future trouble on a gigantic scale.

We have all suffered, especially in the West, from this Roman error. True, their Christianity can take credit for a certain amount of progress in human affairs. Most of this progress, however, is in the material realm. This justifiably allows us to ask: is our modern, machine-dominated world, our super-efficient yet in truth soul-destroying and environmentally devastating 'Paradise', the forbidden fruit of worshipping not Christ but some kind of demigod? With legitimate exasperation, may not at least *some* of us ask: what in the name of God has happened to our beloved Christ and the sublime truth of his Christianity?

One thing is certain: if we want our Christ to rise again it will have to be out of the fertile soil of a new light-filled, knowledge-based faith. To achieve this we will not only have to do some hard, spiritual spadework; we will have to know *where* to dig. We will need to sidestep traditional doctrines and dogmas; we will even have to look beyond the traditional Gospels and the New Testament on which the old dark faith of our ancestors was based. Undoubtedly these latter documents contain valuable truths about the Christ, but during the 19th and 20th centuries they have been dug almost to death. The truth is that this robust exegesis has done far more for the atheists than the believers or the true seekers. It has yielded next to nothing of that ancient light that the modern seeker needs to rekindle in his or her soul in order to truly know the Christ, the light of that great being the Gnostics called Sophia. Catastrophically, she was banished from Christianity with the defeat of the Gnostics. She needs to return. However, the canonical Gospels[1] or the *New Testament* generally are not sufficient to this task. To advance on our journey, therefore, we must turn to the Gnostic texts.

It is only comparatively recently that these ancient texts have come to light, especially with the discovery in the middle of the last century of the Dead Sea Scrolls and the Nag Hammadi Library. The circumstances surrounding these two discoveries indeed bear all the hallmarks of a deliberate attempt by some farsighted individuals to preserve for a distant, future generation (ours!) knowledge of the divine Sophia, knowledge of whom, at the time these texts were hidden away – for by all accounts that is what happened – was being systematically stamped out by the new types of Roman-bred Christians: the dogmatists and the

[1.] The unique nature of the fourth Gospel, John's, necessitates that it always stands alone. This point will be discussed in more detail later in our book, especially in Chapter 8.

heretic hunters. To these types Sophia was far too closely associated with the Goddess of Nature, whose worship and religions they regarded as being in total opposition to their new God, whose image they inevitably based on the Father God of the Jewish religion, out of which their new religion was born. Indeed, these early Roman followers of the Christ feared and hated 'paganism' quite as much as the Jews before them had hated the Gentiles, a tradition of religious jealousy which they also undoubtedly inherited from the Jews. These Roman Catholic Christians did not seem to understand that Christ Jesus was quite simply a different kind of God altogether than vengeful old Jehovah.

The Gnostics knew it, however, and the discovery of their writings presents to us today the opportunity to renew their ancient wisdom. Their writings have the power not only to reshape our Christian history, but to reorient our Christian destiny. They can rid traditional, Roman-inspired Christianity of its rigid dogmatism and awaken consciousness to powerful new levels of understanding. They will, in other words, help clear the way for the modern soul to be awakened and opened once more to the pure, gentle, ancient and very healing light of the Sophia.

For the 'munching masses', this admittedly may be a very slow process. However, for those who hunger for real knowledge, who are eager to initiate in their soul a renewal of the wonderful Mystery of the Christ, the journey must begin here and now.

Perhaps the best known of the Gnostic texts (best known, no doubt, because it was discovered much earlier than those mentioned above) is the *Pistis Sophia*, in which the Christ, during the 40 days between his Resurrection and Ascension, speaks to his disciples at length and in mysterious, highly colourful, even cosmic language about Sophia, a spiritual Being already known to them because they identified her with the soul, or psyche.

Of course, the symbolic language of the *Pistis Sophia* is open to much imaginative interpretation. Fundamentally, however, it represents Sophia as the soul of the human being which has fallen from its original unitary perfection in the bosom of God and must be redeemed. The sages, avatars and initiates of all ages know of and teach about this fallen state of humans. We are unfortunately unfinished animals, very imperfect creatures who nevertheless long for perfection. The great Initiate, Moses, characterises this for the Hebrews in the Paradise story in Genesis. More than any other people, perhaps, the Hebrews longed for atonement and redemption, and expected their Messiah to deliver it. When he eventually came, however, they could not see him. 'He was in the world but the world did not recognize him' (John 1:10).

The ancients always taught that understanding the true nature of the soul was both the key to the universe and to self-knowledge. But we must first acknowledge our fallen state, admit our many faults and failings, and for this to happen, we must *listen* very carefully. Only then can the miracle can occur, for in this very act of listening, atonement – meaning "at-one-ment" is contained. Only when we engage in meditative inner listening can we join with our deeper self and hear the small but clear voice that calls us into the light. This is the same healing light that John spoke of so wonderfully in his Gospel: 'I am the Light of the World' (John, 8:12).

In the *Pistis Sophia*, however, Jesus speaks of his light even more majestically. There, because of his Resurrection, he says it has become a crown of light for Sophia. He goes on to tell of how the joining of these two fabulous lights becomes, for those who follow him, a great new outpouring of divine spiritual Light.

This, of course, is none other than what has been traditionally called the Holy Spirit in the Christian religion. But do the followers of this religion really know what or whom they are talking about? Do they know, in fact, that belief in this Spirit was declared heretical by a Church Council held in Constantinople in 869?[2]

The truth of the matter is that little or nothing is known of the Holy Spirit in mainstream Christianity. All the talk of her there is like an orchestra playing a very bad score on out-of-tune instruments, for she was banished from Christianity long ago. Moreover, her denial caused the Church to become something of a headless monster, as its subsequent appallingly violent and bloody history surely proves. Indeed, the denial of Sophia in mainstream Christianity is the fundamental reason for all the many sins that have been committed in the name of Christ by the Church down the centuries, a Church which, of course, we are soberly reminded, was born out of the belly of the Roman beast.

Only Esoteric Christianity can tackle and overcome this beast. For just as light overcomes darkness, knowledge will always triumph over ignorance.

Sophia, then, is the Guide on the path to the redemption of the human soul. Before the Gnostics, the ancients called

[2] I have dealt with this in detail in Chapter 10 of my book, Esoteric Christianity – A Tragic History. ISBN: 978-0-9540255-5-7

her the Virgin of Light. As the cosmic consort of the Christ, she is the 'key to the Universe', the Door to the Temple of self-knowledge. Socrates, the father of philosophy, knew her, too, albeit by another name. Plato tells us how Socrates, all his life, in all his thinking and doing, was guided by a female spirit Being from higher worlds.

Socrates was ahead of his time. Few understood him. He was put to death for his beliefs and teachings. Christ, too, was a radical teacher. His spiritual message was more potent and powerful than human ears had ever heard, far too powerful for the religious establishment of his own generation. They did not understand him, and he, too, was put to death, for his so-called blasphemies. However, he triumphed, as he said he would, over the dark masters of Death, and he reappeared, and will always reappear to his followers in an incorruptible, ethereal body.

Speaking on the Mount of Olives to his disciples, as he does in the *Pistis Sophia*, Christ makes clear to them what Socrates meant when he, Socrates, spoke of his guide. Christ explained in great detail who or what the Holy Spirit was, and how she redeems and gives new life to the human soul. It was a wonderful message, the most wonderful mankind had ever heard, and because of it, the Christ movement grew in leaps and bounds. All kinds of people were attracted to it. However, as with all social movements, after the early idealistic enthusiasm faded, it began to be infiltrated by ambitious and greedy people whose worldly goals were totally at odds with Christ's basic message. As this infiltration gained momentum, it made way for the eventual hijacking of the movement by that most hard-headed, militaristic people the world has ever known, the Romans.

To give the movement universal or 'catholic' appeal, the Romans reduced the great mysterious river of the Christ to the thinnest of trickles and drip-fed this to the tribal masses of the new, post-imperial Europe, threatening eternal damnation to those who refused to believe. In this way the Christ's teaching and his sacrifice was muddled and muddied out of all recognition, put into the service of human greed for money and power, and the very kernel of it eventually denied in the year 869. Thus, the great spiritual and physical mess the world is in today is due entirely to the Romans and their so-called Christianity.

Sophia, however, is returning in our time. Esoteric Christianity speaks of her clearly. Esoteric Christianity is in fact Sophia-inspired Christianity. She always appears at times of great stress and difficulty in human affairs. She may be known only to a small number of 'Gnostics' at the moment, but that will change, for she is rising like the sun of a grand new dawn. In her hands she carries the Grail of healing and salvation for our troubled planet, our sick humanity. To be healed, all we have to do is open our hearts to her. Then those of us who may, with justifiable pride, call ourselves the 'Children of the Light' will surely come to know and share in the divine promise of Christ: health, happiness and immortality.

CHAPTER 3

THE IMPORTANCE OF IMAGINATION

Christianity in our time needs to be re-learnt. Traditional Christianity has served its purpose. It was based on, and grew out of, a development of the intellect, or the head. Today's Christians, however, need to experience the truth of Christ *in their hearts*. We are not satisfied anymore with simply knowing the Christ or knowing something about him. We need to really *feel* him.

Thinking is primarily an intellectual activity based in the brain, or the head. Feeling, on the other hand, is the province of the heart. Moreover, if pure thinking is akin to the spirit, then feeling is akin to the soul, which envelopes everything concerning our psychic life. Thus if the spirit *thinks*, the soul *feels*, and it does this best through the power of imagination.

Imagination is a great problem for the traditional Church. Its leaders are not only suspicious of it, but greatly fear it. A mystery unto itself, the imagination is nonetheless a powerful tool for knowledge, for it is the language of the soul. The Gnostics knew this and worked with it. As a result, they were far more imaginative in their understanding of the Christ than the hard-headed literalists who vehemently opposed them. There was indeed a great battle between the open-hearted Gnostics and the hard-headed literalists in the first couple of centuries of the Christian era. However, led by militant Rome, the literalists eventually won the day and took over the movement completely.

This elimination of Gnostic Christianity was a great error on the part of the Christian leadership. The time has now come, however, to reinstate the imagination into Christianity. This is one of main tasks of Esoteric Christianity.

It is not an easy task. For the imagination is like a garden which, if uncared for, grows wild, and whose flowers then, no matter how beautiful, will be smothered and choked by brambles and weeds.

A wild imagination, therefore, is not only bad for the soul, but bad also for the spirit of the soul's heavenly origins, and the body of its earthly foundation. As the child of our 'heavenly father' and 'earthly mother', the soul needs to be cared for. This primarily means education. Moreover, that education must be undertaken in the language of the soul itself: the imagination. Modern education pays little more than lip service to the imagination. Modern education is focussed mainly on the development of the intellect on the one hand and of the physical body on the other. The care of the soul, if indeed this is recognized as an educational need at all, is left to religion. Oh, undoubtedly for Christians the Church was able to care for and nourish the soul to some degree in the past. But that day is gone. The Church's teaching and moral power, long in decline, recently has all but vanished for most thinking people, Christian or otherwise. So where does that leave the 'munching masses' for whom one can say the Church was originally established? In a spiritual no man's land.

Although the physical body of the average Western person today is well fed, indeed often overfed, their soul is like a prowling, hungry, lone wolf, scouring for food in a squalid, spiritual wasteland. The modern soul is simply starving to death.

The reality is that if the human soul receives any kind of food at all nowadays it comes mostly from that ubiquitous and highly seductive 'tin god' one finds in almost every room of every modern house, and even in the hands of little children: the electronic screen. For here is a universal god who, tragically and ironically, receives more willing worship than any other god in human history. Yet with 'his' myriad forms, faces and figures, with 'his' universal promotion of violence, greed, glamour and pornography, 'he' perpetually mocks all human values and virtues. Anyone whose spiritual eye is open even to a small degree can easily see that this god does not feed the soul at all, but rather is slowly poisoning her to death with excrement.

We have to remember, of course, that we created this

'thing'. It therefore follows that if we are to be saved from its deal of spiritual death, we must also do it ourselves. Actually, in the modern world we are faced with a momentous choice: the life or death of the soul. In the past, the Church took it upon itself to foster the life of the soul. Nowadays, however, that institution acts more like a cold shadow than a healing light. If you want to save your soul in the modern climate you must be pro-active and diligently take up the practise of individual self-development. In spiritual terms, self-development is based on self-discipline, which leads to self-knowledge.

This self-knowledge can eventually lead to what the eminent psychologist Carl Jung called 'individuation'. The reality is that consciously undertaken spiritual self-development leads to the forming of a new soul faculty. Even prior to Jung, the German idealist philosopher Fichte was aware of this. In his book, *The Science of Knowledge*, published in 1813, he described 'the existence of a quite new inner sensory organ through which a new world is opened up, a world that simply does not exist for the ordinary person'. This new faculty of the modern, self-conscious soul is based primarily on a development of the imagination. We are not speaking here of fantasy, daydreaming and the like, of course, but of a wide-awake moral faculty which does not depend on reason or intellect alone for gaining knowledge. This can also become a clairvoyant faculty in which our essential self, our human Ego, can quite consciously step outside the familiar box of our purely material world and into the mysterious spiritual world that in reality forms the foundation of our thinking. This surrounds us always, of course, but we know little of it except through occasional flashes of intuition or inspiration or perhaps through the shadows it casts into our night-life of dreams.

The primary tool for the development of this modern self-conscious soul faculty is *meditation*, about which we will say more later. Now, however, we must pause on our journey to consider a principle which was fundamental to the practice of early Christianity, but which, with the defeat of Gnosticism, disappeared from it along with much else. We speak of *initiation*. It is another of the tasks of modern Esoteric Christianity to reinstate this principle and make it central once more to the pursuit of true knowledge of the Christ Being.

CHAPTER 4

INITIATION

Nietzsche was wrong: God is not dead. For the genuine
spiritual seeker, however, the Christianity that grew
out of the belly of the Roman beast most certainly is.

Roman Christianity has all but killed the Christ. It is
only through Esoteric Christianity, and the deep love and
knowledge of the Christ that it kindles in the human heart
and soul, that Christianity in any form can survive into the
future.

Esoteric Christianity attempts to understand the core
aspects, knowledge and teachings of the very early
Christian movement, and evaluates, updates and reinstates
these for the genuine seeker of the Christ in our time.

The early Christian movement was heavily influenced,
as already stated, not only by the Hebrew Mysteries but also

by the Mystery Religions of Greece and the Near East. This fact is easily deduced from depictions of Christ in the catacombs, for instance as a shepherd – a distinct reference to the Greek god Hermes. He is also depicted as Helios, the sun god, and even as Bacchus, the god of wine.

The enthusiastic seekers after gnosis in those far-off days came from many different spiritual streams. They were attracted to the Christ for myriad reasons, but chiefly because they saw in him someone who miraculously combined, unified and harmonized the cosmic multiplicity of the gods of the many Mystery cults into a single *historical personality*. This surely was a god with a difference!

In the birth, life, death and most importantly, the Resurrection of Jesus, not only the enthusiastic seekers after spiritual knowledge, but *everybody* could see that the sacred but secret drama of the Mysteries had moved out of the Temples and onto the stage of human history. Before this, the gods were known to the masses only in a superficial or even superstitious way. Jesus changed all that.

The central ritual act of the Temple rites in all the ancient Mysteries required the hierophant to put the chela, or pupil, into a sleep similar to death. There was, of course, a long preparation for this, a preparation which could last for many years. However, when the time came for this, the final act of initiation, the pupil was put into a death-like state which lasted for three days. During that time, under the guidance of the hierophant, the pupil inhabited the spiritual world. Then, when awoken by the hierophant, the pupil was reborn as a new initiate. Now possessed of full knowledge of the higher or spiritual worlds, he or she received a new name to mark this transformation. The name was taken from a list of previous initiates of the particular Temple where the pupil received instruction, initiates who had passed the threshold and now numbered among the illustrious Dead.

Jesus was familiar with all the ancient Mystery rites and cults of his time. He travelled widely as a young man and was initiated into many of them. In some amazing lectures given at the beginning of the 20th century, the great modern initiate, Rudolf Steiner, spoke of how in the body of Jesus of Nazareth there lived the reincarnated individuality of Zarathustra, the ancient Persian prophet, and how in a sense he re-experienced many of the initiations of his earlier incarnations on his travels. (We will come back to this in Chapter 5.) However, as indicated clearly in John's Gospel, Jesus' Baptism by John in the Jordan was a unique kind of initiation. This is best indicated by the new name he received: Christos, a Greek word meaning 'the anointed one'. For the Gnostics, Jesus was, at his Baptism, anointed with the 'fullness of the divinity' which they called the Pleroma (as discussed in Chapter 7). Whereas in all previous initiations the initiand, i.e. the one being initiated, although reborn, remained a human being, in this Baptism of Jesus of Nazareth by John, Jesus the man became Christ Jesus the God. That is why the festival celebrating this baptism in the Church calendar is called Epiphany, a Greek word with the root meaning of 'a divine manifestation'.

Acutely aware of his destiny, even before his Baptism, as the incarnation of the long-prophesied Messiah, from his Baptism onwards Jesus speaks not simply as a prophet - that is, not simply *for* God, but *as* God. Therefore, he now openly and boldly declares: 'My Father and I are one' (John

10:30). The learned Jews of the Temple of course regarded
this as blasphemy of the first degree and stoned him. But
that didn't stop Jesus from continuing to make his unique
proclamation. He went about Palestine like a God, working
miracles, castigating the hypocritical, empty, religious rites
of the orthodox Jewish sects and railing at how they had
turned the 'house of his Father' into little more than a
butcher's abattoir or a changing room for moneylenders. In
a scene of unparalleled fury, he enters the Temple and with
'a whip of chords drove all the dealers out' (John 2:14-16).
He actually declares *himself* to be the Temple! 'Pull it down
and I will rebuild it in three days' (Matthew 26:61). The old
and secret ways of the Temple, he manifestly says, are over.
From now on, 'I am the Way' (John 14:6).

Jesus feels it is his unique task not only to bring the *I
Am* God of his forefathers out of the confines of the Jewish
Temple, but to make him known to *all* peoples. No longer is
this God to be the possession only of a 'chosen few', of those
who could enter the 'holy of holies' or partake of the
initiation rites of the Temple. Jesus says 'to all who have
ears to hear' that through his sacrificial life and death,
everyone will be enabled to participate in initiation.

The most spectacular and controversial miracle Jesus
performed was in truth a demonstration of this: the raising
of Lazarus. Here on an open, public stage he did something
which, up until then, had only been done behind the
secretive walls of the Temple.

In John's Gospel Lazarus is described as a rich young
disciple of Jesus who failed to do what Jesus asked, i.e. to
give away all his riches. Lazarus later became ill, and his
sisters turned to Jesus, who had already healed many

people, for help. But Jesus did not help him. In fact, he let him die, having a higher purpose in mind for his death, through which he planned to demonstrate his power as a great and entirely new type of hierophant.

When, soon after the death of Lazarus, his sister Mary scolded Jesus for letting her brother die, Jesus knew it was the time to act. Ensuring that a large crowd had gathered around the tomb of Lazarus, he sought out the spirit of Lazarus in the spiritual world and performed the ritual act of waking the disciple from the death-sleep:

> 'Then he raised his voice in a great cry: "Lazarus come forth." The dead man came out, his hands and feet swathed in linen bands, his face wrapped in a cloth. Jesus said, "Loose him. Set him free." '
> (John 11:43-44).[3]

It is highly significant that it was precisely because of this ritual act that the Sanhedrin decided to kill Jesus, whom they perceived as betraying their Mysteries. 'From that moment on they plotted to kill Jesus' (John 11:53).

As the story of Lazarus makes clear, from the time of John's baptism of Jesus initiation takes on a completely new form and meaning. The Gnostics knew this and built their teaching and their schools around it. Christ Jesus was for them not only the new God of mankind, but the new Temple *and* its hierophant. They knew that all spiritual knowledge must now be focussed on the divine Light of the *I Am*, as revealed by the new Godman, Christ Jesus, who declared, '*I Am* the Light of the world.' (John 8:12).

---

[3] For a much deeper exploration of the meaning of this miracle, see Chapter 8.

However, after the elimination of the Gnostics from the Church, the pursuit of this new Christ initiation was outlawed. As self-knowledge, it implied a spiritual and moral freedom that severely threatened the Church's expansionist policy, which derived from the centralist and imperialist ideologies it had inherited from Rome. So, from this point onwards, true knowledge of the Christ automatically became esoteric knowledge.

The pursuit of this kind of knowledge never completely disappeared, however. It went underground, and was cultivated by small, isolated, mystical groups, such as the Rosicrucians.

Significantly, it was from these groups also that the wonderful story of the Grail emerged. From about the beginning of the 2nd millennium onwards, for esoteric Christians the Cup of the Last Supper became the focus of their deepest spiritual meditations. More and more clearly the truly seeking ones saw that the blood of the Great Sacrifice of the Christ was not merely the blood of an animal or a man, as was always the case in previous religious sacrifices, but the blood of a *god*. More and more clearly they understood that through the Christ's sacrifice the entire meaning, purpose and very history of the Earth and its peoples had changed. Christ Jesus had become the planetary spirit! From the very Earth he had created a new Vessel and had impregnated it with a truly divine substance. The Earth had received a new aura.

This in a nutshell was the mystique of the Grail which deeply inspired esoteric Christians of the Middle Ages. It was a continuation, a Western development of how the Hellenic Gnostics first saw Jesus. More importantly, however, it is how we must learn to see him again.

In the 77th logia of the Gnostic Gospel of Thomas, Jesus says to his disciples,

> *'I am the light that is over all things. I am all. From me all came forth, and to me all extends. Split a piece of wood, and I am there. Lift up a stone and you will find me there.'*

The direction that Jesus is giving his disciples here is obvious. It is to seek him *actively* in the world. He is drawing a distinction between outer activity and activity carried on behind the secluded walls of a temple, or for that matter a monastery, the latter being the modern equivalent of the temple.

He does not mean, of course, that we should give up the worthy practices of spiritual study, meditation or prayer, but rather that these must now be carried on in conjunction with our work in the world at large. Whatever we do, whatever our occupation or *pro*fession, this must now become our Christian *con*fession. In a nutshell, it does not matter anymore to what family, tribe, country, race, religion or church we belong; it is in the very forming of our *personality* that we now find the Christ, for he has become the manner, matter and means of our Christ initiation.

Moreover, the need for initiation or pure spiritual enlightenment is far greater in our time than it was for the Gnostics. For the forces that work against the spirit have never been greater than they are in our time, so that for many people, simple faith or belief in Christ is no longer sufficient to sustain a healthy inner or psychic life.

In Christian terms, the embodiment of these opposing forces is often called Antichrist. In art or imaginative literature this being is represented in many ways, typically as a kind of humanized beast, beautiful or ugly. Whatever form it takes, however, we may properly regard Antichrist as the great *deceiver* of humankind, a kind of archetypal demon who works with powerful psychic force in the subconscious depths of the human soul. If ignorantly courted, this being is capable of inspiring highly addictive bestial thoughts which can corrupt the moral power of the imagination, and to such a degree that the unsuspecting can be sucked into madness. Such corrupting thoughts are fed and fattened by the decadence and hedonism which is rampant in our time. The enthusiastic modern seeker after true spiritual knowledge should keep this firmly in mind. More than any others, he or she needs strong mental discipline if the great seductive deception of materialism is to be overcome.

But if we are dedicated and sincere in our Quest for the Grail of initiation, that is, for pure, true and genuine spiritual knowledge, we can rest assured that we are well guarded, for within or behind our sense-perceptible world there stands a great and good Spirit of Light.

To thread the path of knowledge to this Spirit means cultivating self-knowledge, which leads to the Christ initiation. For, as previously stated, modern initiation is initiation of the *I Am*, which is the true name of Christ. In John's Gospel, Christ extolls his followers to elaborate the truth of his name in seven profound, mantric mediations. In the third of these he says, '*I Am* the Door' (John 10:9). Here he is speaking of the Door to the heavenly Temple which he opened for human beings through his sacrificial death on Earth. We share in this sacrificial death by sincerely following him. This most certainly is not death worship, but it's very opposite. It is self-liberation. For through the Christ initiation we are awakened to a higher life.

Initially we are awakened to the ethereal presence of our Angel, who is our true or Higher Self, and behind whom always stands the Christ. It must be stated, however, that to achieve this level of initiation requires hard, disciplined work. There are no easy or 'magic' means to it. Esoteric Christianity offers no simple formulae, whether of words, thoughts or exercises, for enlightenment. Rather, it states in all honesty that in order simply to cope nowadays, in order simply to have decent physical and mental health, which is the true wealth, knowledge of the Christ spirit needs to be not only cultivated, but more actively and conscientiously cultivated than ever was the case before.

Knowledge is what the modern soul desires most of all. However, knowledge as we mean it here is more than mere information. In Esoteric Christianity, Christ represents the being, the very *life* of knowledge.

Although this Christ is the free gift of God's Son to the 'munching masses', generally speaking nowadays he is shunned. Consumerist materialism is the modern religion of the traditional 'flock', and it has pushed them into an epidemic of food abuse, drug addiction, homophobia and mental illness. To avoid falling into this trap requires self-knowledge, and self-knowledge is Christ-knowledge. Christ is the universal, archetypal Healer of mankind. To acquire his healing, however, we need to know him, to *really* know him in the initiatory sense outlined above, and this requires constant, hard inner and outer work.

That said, there is a great reward in store for all who take up the path of modern self-initiation. Through it we find the meaning of life, for truly Christ *is* the meaning of life. In the sixth of John's meditations on the *I Am* name, Christ says, '*I Am* the way, the truth and the life' (John, 14:6). Moreover, this Christ is the Son of the supreme creator God we find at the heart of all true religion and spiritual paths.

In this sense, Esoteric Christianity is a path that unifies all religions. There is no question about it. Esoteric Christianity is *the* spiritual path of our time, the one most suited to the needs of the modern searching soul.

CHAPTER 5

ZARATHUSTRA

In the previous chapter we alluded to the fact that before he received his great initiation through his baptism by John in the Jordan, Jesus bore within him the individuality historically known as Zarathustra. In other words, Jesus was a reincarnation of Zarathustra.

Here it must be emphatically stated that while it is unnecessary to *believe* in reincarnation, if you wholeheartedly desire the modern Christ initiation you must not close your mind to it. For many Westerners this can be difficult, for there is in us an historic, culturally conditioned prejudice against the idea of reincarnation. Easterners, by contrast, take it as a fact of life. The reason for the Western prejudice is undoubtedly the Church's long-term anathematization of the doctrine, which is directly related to its early hostility to, and elimination of, the Gnostics who supported and taught it. However, that it is 'unchristian' to believe in reincarnation is pure myth and fallacy. For instance, Origen, one of the original Fathers of the Church who lived during the last phase of the Gnosis, actually taught it. The reason for this is undoubtedly connected with Origen's own teacher and master, Clement of Alexandria, who was a pupil of the Mysteries before he came to Christ, and reincarnation was always taught in the Mysteries.

Even the canonical Gospels attest to the truth of reincarnation, for Jesus himself says that John the Baptist is a reincarnation of the greatest of the Jewish prophets, Elijah. In Matthew 11:14, he unequivocally states to his intimate disciples, 'John is Elijah.'

Who, then, was Zarathustra? A Persian by birth, he is historically regarded as the founder of what is perhaps the world's oldest religion, Zoroastrianism. Zoroaster is the name the ancient Greeks gave him, and it means 'golden star.' Zarathustra's teachings have influenced virtually all the main world religions, right up to modern times. His part in Esoteric Christianity is vital. In fact, understanding the relationship of Jesus to Zarathustra is key to unlocking the secrets of the Christ initiation. These secrets were known to the Gnostics. When the Gnostics were banned, however, this secret knowledge went underground and was cultivated only by small, scattered, esoteric groups. The time now demands that this knowledge be made public.

Contemporary scholarship dates Zarathustra to around the time of the enlightened Persian King, Cyrus the Great (6th century BC). However, classical writers and scholars held that the founder of the Persian religion lived thousands of years earlier than this. For instance, Plutarch (c. 46-120 AD) wrote in his book about Isis and Osiris that 'Zoroaster the magus is said to have lived 5000 years before the Trojan War'. Zoroastrians have always believed in reincarnation. Nowadays they are called Parsees. Their head in Teheran has 'said that 7 Zarathustras appeared in the course of history of which the first lived around 6000 BC and the last in the 6th century BC'.[4] By the 6th century BC the ancient Persian culture and civilization had evolved into what is nowadays called the Achaemenid Empire, which was created by the above-mentioned Cyrus who is also reputed to have been a pupil of Zarathustra.

Zarathustra is historically known by a number of slightly different names and at the time in question was called Nazarathos. He was also a great teacher of the Jews who at this time were held in captivity in one of the main cities of the Achaemenid Empire: Babylon. This is known in Jewish history as the Babylonian Captivity and it began some time before Cyrus came to power. Cyrus, however, released the Jews and allowed them to return to Jerusalem to rebuild their Temple which had earlier been destroyed. Cyrus's actions were undoubtedly due to Zarathustra's influence. All of this points to a very close and vital connection between Zarathustra and the Jews.

In fact, according to Steiner, Zarathustra was long planning to incarnate among the Jews in order to prepare and provide a physical vessel for the Christ eventually to incarnate. For in one of his earlier incarnations, the one in which he founded the Persian religion, Zarathustra became

[4] *Zarathustra – The First Prophet of Christ*, by D.J. van Bemmelen, 1968. Privately published.

aware that the great Sun God, whom he called Ahura Mazdao,[5] later to be called the Logos or the Christ, was eventually going to incarnate in a physical body on the Earth. This cosmic Being, exalted above all others, then became the focus of all Zarathustra's spiritual and sacrificial work on Earth, for he wanted to offer *himself* as fully as was humanly possible to this great Being. This required a very long preparation and is alluded to in Matthew's Gospel in the lineage given there of Jesus, which is traced back, in a kind of multi-branched, cabbalistic 'tree of life', through Solomon, David and ultimately to Abraham.

To avoid confusion, it should be remembered that all of these incarnations refer only to the purely *physical* body. However, when we speak of reincarnation, we speak fundamentally of the spirit-self or the Ego of the human being. Thus, while Zarathustra did not, as far as we know, physically incarnate in any of the forebears of Jesus mentioned in Matthew, the whole development is guided from the spiritual world by him, who, as a very lofty spiritual, almost angelic, individuality, is able to accomplish such things. He himself did not need to incarnate in any of these physical sheaths and is therefore not mentioned in the lineage. He did, however, incarnate about 100 years before his Jesus of Nazareth incarnation, when he was known as Jesu ben Pandira. Understandably, in exoteric literature this earlier incarnation is often mixed up with Christ Jesus, for as Jesu ben Pandira, Zarathustra was also a great teacher, and also suffered a similar fate as the Christ did. Esoteric Christianity, however, knows Jesu ben Pandira to

---

[5] Ahura Mazdao can be translated as the 'aura of the sun'. In those far-off times, the priest initiate of the Mystery wisdom could actually feel the nearness of God in his or her subtle or soul body, and because of this could communicate with God clairvoyantly and prophetically.

be primarily the great Righteous Teacher of the Essenes.

The Essenes were an ascetic sect who flourished during Jesus's life and to whom he was naturally very drawn, as also was John the Baptist. Moreover, the Essenes were a reconstituted, contemporary development of a sect Nazarathos himself had long previously established, probably during or soon after the Babylonian Captivity, when he was physically incarnated and was known by the name Nazarathos. The sect was then called the Nazarites and were presumably founded as a preparation for Zarathustra's future incarnations among the Jews.

Unlike the Levites, the Nazarites were a lay community with their own special Law which is outlined in great detail in the Old Testament Book of Numbers, Chapter 6. Also unlike the Levites, they came from different tribes. They were ascetics who practised various disciplines such as not cutting their hair, not drinking wine etc. In other words, they cultivated the inner path of initiation. As the name Nazareth implies, they had a large community in this town. Thus, in the Nativity story of Jesus, as it is told in Matthew's Gospel, it is only natural that this Zarathustra Jesus, on his return to Palestine from Egypt, where his parents took him in order to escape the 'massacre of the innocents' by the wicked King Herod, would go to the safest possible place, a place in a sense he himself had established in a previous incarnation: Nazareth.

Thus we can say that Jesus of Nazareth is a lofty individuality who, although human, is as near to an angel as a human being can become while yet remaining human. He is capable of, and indeed has made, many great sacrifices before his Jesus of Nazareth incarnation. In this particular incarnation, however, through the instrument of John, he is able to perform the greatest sacrifice of all in that he offers up to God his own body of flesh, the most beautiful and perfect physical body that ever existed on Earth.

In effect, at the moment of his Baptism by John, Jesus of Nazareth absolutely vacates his physical body and returns voluntarily to the spiritual world, so that the supreme or archetypal Self of the World, the One we call the Christ, could enter the physical world in a human body. Special and very long preparation for this Event was required, for a divine being cannot ever fully enter an ordinary human body; if that were to happen, the body would simply explode. Thus, only the body of Jesus of Nazareth was able to receive the Christ Divinity. Thus, we have the unique phenomenon of a divine Being inhabiting a purely human body.

This great Being, called the Logos in John's Gospel, is also said to be consubstantial with the Father Ground of the World, and is therefore also correctly called the Son of God.

Mainstream Christianity absolutely ignores these esoteric facts and actually smothers John's Baptism of Jesus in a cloud of sectarian and theological jargon which often does more to put people off Christ than onto him. Esoteric Christianity, on the other hand, speaks plain and straight. Its purpose is to stimulate the mind and soul of the genuine seeker into searching for the truth, the real truth of the Christ. Thus, Esoteric Christianity is for those who are not content with outworn dogmas, rigid formulas of dead, printed words, or abstruse theological jargon. It speaks the *living truth* that, in the human being who bears the name of Christ, there also lives the forces of the exalted and divine

Sun Being in whom every human Ego finds its origin.

This is the Solar Logos of the World of whom John speaks so profoundly in his Gospel. As stated in previous chapters, in cultivating this esoteric knowledge we are also cultivating true knowledge of our deepest self, of our own spirit Ego which has been given new incarnational life by Christ. To get to know this extrasensory entity is the ultimate goal of all genuine spiritual striving. The reward of this striving is great, the greatest, in fact, that the world can offer, for to know one's true Self is also to be at peace with God.

Esoteric Christianity allows the human being to become capable of recognizing in an intimate, true and living manner God who became man. Christ Jesus for us then becomes the source of all wisdom, opening our vision and bestowing on us understanding of both the natural and the spiritual world. As a consequence we are also given that which knows no name. This is the Peace of Christ that the great Initiate Paul wrote about in his Letter to the Philippians, the Peace 'that passes all understanding' (Phil 4-7).

CHAPTER 6

THE TWO JESUS CHILDREN

Yeou may have noticed that in the previous chapter I used
the designation 'Jesus of Nazareth' only in particular
contexts. There is a very good reason for this. It relates to
the otherwise inexplicable fact that we have reported in the
canonical Gospels two completely different genealogies for
the Jesus child. Biblical scholars have pickled their brains
in an effort to explain this glaring anomaly, perhaps the
most controversial of all the exegetical problems of the
synoptic Gospels but have nevertheless failed because they
do not possess the key.

You will presently learn what this key is.

Firstly, only the Gospels of Matthew and Luke give a
family tree of Jesus. Both Mark's and John's Gospel
completely ignore it and begin their account of that unique

and sacred life with Jesus's momentous initiation: the Baptism by John in the Jordan. For the ancestry of Jesus, therefore, we must look to Matthew and Luke. But while they both trace the ancestry back as far as King David, Matthew does it through David's son, Solomon, while Luke does it through another of David's sons, Nathan. The result is the impossible claim of two totally different genealogies for the same child.

The only logical explanation is that Matthew and Luke are writing about different children.

A preliminary explanation of this anomaly is associated with 'the messianic factor' underpinning the Jewish religion. From about the 8th century BC onwards there arose among the Jews the idea that a man would eventually be born to them who would become not only their own Saviour but Saviour of the entire world. We must remember that the very concept of Israel had arisen out of the deepest possible otherworldly impulses, upon which the great Initiate of the ancient, sacred Mysteries, Moses, founded and formed the Jewish nation and religion. In this the priests ruled, the prophets chastised and the judges judged. But the people, unruly from the very beginning, became so ungovernable due to their constant deviation from, and sinning against, the law of God that it seemed almost impossible that they would ever be redeemed. It was, however, the visionary power of their prophets, especially Isiah, that kept the whole amazing enterprise alive and gave it *some* hope of success. For it was Isiah who foresaw the coming of a man who through his own self-sacrifice would save both Israel and the world from annihilation by the wrath of God. This man, says Isiah, would be named Immanuel, meaning 'God is with us'. He would rectify all outstanding wrongs and instigate a whole new world order where 'the wolf shall live with the sheep . . . the cow and the bear shall be friends . . . the infant shall play over the hole of the cobra, and the young child over the viper's nest' (Isiah 11:6-8).

This was the Messiah. He was the potential incarnation or human embodiment of an ideal that encompassed the whole of creation and inspired the vision of a world where pure spiritual love permeated not only all human beings, but animals, plants and the very soil itself. However, as time passed, the geo-political realities that the Jews as a nation had constantly to face threatened to completely undermine the tremendous spiritual vision of the prophets. Thus, only with great reluctance, as the Bible clearly shows, did Israel eventually succumb to the more worldly power of kings and agree to be ruled by them. Whereas they had always conceived of their coming Messiah in a spiritual or otherworldly way, they now had to consider him (and of course he had to be male!) in a worldly or kingly way also. It was this kind of thinking that gave rise to the difficult idea of two messiahs, one kingly and the other priestly, and it must have influenced the Gospel writers as they attempted to, as it were, explain Jesus as the Messiah to the masses, for that was the prime purpose of the Gospels.

If you read Matthew's Gospel alongside Luke's with this 'twin-messiah theology' in mind, you will see that Matthew clearly has the kingly Messiah in mind, whereas Luke focusses on the priestly one. For instance, at the very opening of his account, after he has given the genealogical tree and related the birth of Jesus, Matthew paints his famous picture of the Three Wise Men who travelled a long distance from the East in order to pay homage to Jesus at his birth. Matthew tells us that these men were astrologers (although significantly, they are regarded traditionally as kings also) who had seen a new star in the sky. Careful astrological calculations led them to believe that the appearance of this star heralded the fulfilment of an old prophesy, long known to them, that a powerful new *king* was to be born on Earth (Matthew 2:2). They felt compelled to pay him homage, and the star itself actually guided them to the place of his birth, Bethlehem.

The kingly theme continues in Matthew, where it is soon revealed that the child is the potential victim of an evil king: Herod. The parents then must flee the country and go to the 'land of kings', Egypt, in order to save their child. And of course, in the genealogy of Jesus with which Matthew opens his book, the child Jesus is descended from the wisest of all the Jewish kings, Solomon.

By contrast, when we turn to Luke's Gospel, we find that our attention is continually directed to the more spiritual aspect of the child's life, especially in the way that the priesthood and the Temple are emphasised. Thus, early in his Gospel Luke goes into great detail about a priest called Zechariah who, we are told, was promised by the Archangel Gabriel that, despite being of advanced age, his wife would bear him a son. This child is John the Baptist. Later in this Gospel an event is described in the Temple which is in fact the aforementioned key to the whole new Mystery of the Christ, and which we will presently explain.

There are, however, no *explicit* references to the twin-messiah in the Gospels and only veiled references in the Old Testament. The existence of the theology only came fully to light with the discovery in the 19th century of the gnostic text, the *Pistis Sophia*, and more especially with the unearthing in the middle of the last century of a long-hidden library of the Essenes in the caves of Qumran, generally known as the Dead Sea Scrolls. David Ovason, in his excellent, hugely informative and scholarly book on the subject, *The Two Children*,[6] asserts after a detailed examination of the Qumran texts: 'It should be clear by now that the Essene literature discovered at Qumran was permeated with the expectation of two Messiahs, or anointed ones.'

There were many Essene communities during Jesus's time, and similar communities had been in existence for decades, or even centuries, before him. As indicated in the previous chapter, they were a modern development of an older ascetic Jewish Order called the Nazarites and they spiritually cultivated, in a highly ritualized lifestyle, the messianic knowledge and expectation. Thus, when eventually the story of the Death and Resurrection of Jesus became well known, they and their associates made every effort to reconcile the 'twin-messiah theology' with this unique Event. The Gospel writers would undoubtedly have been very familiar with the Essenes, their writings and their teachings Whether or not Luke and Matthew were complicit in their confirmation of the 'twin-messiah theology', their different genealogies of the Jesus child prove it beyond doubt.

However, in trying to understand this Mystery and the many questions the 'twin-theology' raises, we must first take note of the fact that in the first place all four of the

[6] *The Two Children*, by David Ovason, Century, 2001

canonical Gospel writers wanted simply to tell a story. This indeed is what primarily distinguishes the Gospels from the Gnostic texts, which are more concerned with theology and spiritual instruction. The canonical writers considered theology or religious or spiritual instruction to be secondary to their overall purpose, which was to produce a memorable or impressionable *narrative*. The word "Gospel" actually means 'good news'. Thus, the Evangelists primarily had a 'good news story' to tell. Their books therefore we can consider as reportage, albeit of a unique nature, due to the unique Event they describe. Here, as with all popular reports, complexity is wisely sacrificed to simplicity, in order to convey the overall message.

Thus, the canonical Gospels tell the story seemingly of one person whom we know as Christ Jesus and who is the God of all Christians, esoteric or otherwise. However complex their own knowledge and understanding of the great Event was, the Gospel writers were nevertheless deeply conscious of their primary task, which was to write a story about the Event sufficient to the needs of the average person, that is, sufficient to awaken in them faith and belief in the new God, Christ Jesus.

That was the challenge. John succeeds in it best, because he knew Jesus best. He is referred to explicitly in the Gospel as the 'one whom Jesus loved', and you will understand better why he is thus referred to after reading Chapter 8 in this book.

Thus we can see that in early Christianity, faith for the masses was considered more important than knowledge. In many places in the Gospels, Jesus rails against the unbelievers. If he was able to hate at all, it was primarily directed against the atheists and their atheism, for they denied and abused the truth of the Great Spirit whom he called his Father. After his Resurrection and a short time before he returns to the heavenly world of his Father, Jesus instructs his disciples to 'Feed my sheep' (John 10:9). The Word of the Gospel had to be fed to *everyone* on Earth. '*I Am* the Bread of Life' (John 6:35). In a similar vein, at the end of Mark's Gospel Jesus instructs his disciples to 'Go forth to every part of the world and proclaim the Good News to the whole earth' (Mark 16:15).

We have already shown how the very early Church was gnostic in character. But this was true only in the sense that there were those who *knew* the complexity of the great Event, and those who were merely followers of those who knew. In other words, there were shepherds and sheep. The knowledge element was, as far as possible, kept carefully apart from the 'flock', the faithful. Only if you were very special would you receive instruction in the deeper secrets of the Christ Mystery. It was a practice that was carried over into the young Christian movement from the old Mysteries.

John's text, like the other Gospels, is meant primarily to inspire faith, but it is more important than the other Gospels in the sense that it stands as a doorway into the Mystery of the Christ Being: '*I Am* the Door' (John 10:9). The Mystery is, of course, inevitably alluded to in the great and exciting business of spreading the Gospel Word to the masses, but its complexity, its *gnosis*, is kept back because of the correctly perceived danger of it interfering with the Word's more important task of inspiring *faith*. Back then it was not necessary to *know* it in order to have faith. If, however, you acquired enough faith, you would be led through the Door and became a Christian Initiate, as distinct from any other kind of Initiate, of whom there were many at that time, mainly because by then the old Mysteries had become far less strict in their admittance criteria and had in many ways become decadent.

Christianity changed all that. The early dictum of the Christian teachers was: 'Believe, that you may know.' Faith for the masses was prioritised over knowledge. However, as a species we have come on a long way since then, especially in respect of our thinking, or our ability to know. This is due, initially, to the influence of Hellenism and Greek thought and philosophy generally on the new Christian movement. Focussing on the great Mystery Event as knowledge of it was handed down orally by the Initiates and written about by Christ's disciples and others, thinking continued to develop and strengthen in the West right up to the German Idealists of the 19th century. Alas, after Hegel, by and large thinking turned away from the spiritual aspect of the world and focussed more and more on the physical. The end result, however, is that today we can think about complexities with a cold and calculated strength, and an intellectual acumen undreamt of by the early Christians. For this reason, in our time it is far more appropriate when approaching the Christ Mystery to be guided not by the old dictum 'Believe, that you may know', but by its reversal: 'Know, that you may believe.'

This can be very difficult for many people, of course, but only because of the terrible ignorance that was visited upon Christianity by the Roman Church. With the defeat of Gnosticism in the 3rd and 4th centuries, a disturbing arrogance invaded the Christian intellect, an arrogance that came to its most forceful expression in the famous and hugely influential writer and bishop, Augustine of Hippo. From his period onwards, until roughly the 5th century, the Church began to apply the old 'believe' dictum to the absolute exclusion of knowledge. They forced the faith upon the masses and did it with such violence that they almost completely annihilated the Mystery of Christ in the process. To believe in the Mystery became heretical. You got burnt at the stake for it in the Middle Ages, if your beliefs became known. However, despite all this, Esoteric Christianity has kept knowledge of the true spirit of Christ alive down the dark centuries, thanks mainly to John and his followers, so that today, happily, it can be revived.

Esoteric Christianity categorically affirms that there were two Jesus children, one born to the Solomon line of descent as described by Matthew, and another to the Nathan line as described by Luke. Guided by a wise Providence, both children were born roughly around the same time and both had parents called Mary and Joseph, which names, like Jesus, were also very common at this time among the Jews. Both sets of parents also lived in or near the town of Nazareth, but while the Luke or Nathan Jesus was an only child, the Solomon Jesus had siblings.

As previously indicated, complex and very careful preparations were made from the spiritual world for all these events to occur, preparations in which Zarathustra was the key *human* agent. However, through a *divine* agent, that is, through the Christ, the two children became one. An understanding of how this union is accomplished through a Temple initiation, which is briefly but very significantly described in Luke, and which we will presently address directly, is key to the great Mystery of the human Incarnation of the divine Christ. Through this union Isiah's prophecy comes true: God in Christ becomes one with us and is in us. We merely have to learn to awaken him.

Knowledge awakens! We have already seen how Zarathustra had known from his very early incarnation, thousands of years before Christ, beginning in the ancient Persian civilization, of the coming of the Solar Logos, or the great Sun Spirit to the Earth. Thus, when Zarathustra eventually incarnated as Jesus of Nazareth, he brought with him in his Ego, that is, in his individual human spirit-self, all the knowledge, both physical and spiritual, it was possible for a human being to have at that time. To distinguish him from the Luke child, he may therefore be called the Child of Wisdom. Matthew gives details of his eventful birth and childhood up to the time he settles with his parents in the town of Nazareth.

The events described involving the Luke child are quite different. They are much more human and down-to-earth. It is for this reason that Luke's has traditionally been the most favoured of the canonical Gospels. It tells a very heart-warming story. The appearance of the angels to the shepherds informing them of the child's birth in a stable is in direct contrast to the cosmic feeling we get from Matthew's account, where a bright star appears in the sky to the three wise astrologers, informing them of the birth of a great new king who would be infinitely wiser than themselves. The Luke child, by contrast, seems like the personification of purest innocence. Of this child Steiner significantly says that it had no earthly karma, that he was incarnating for the *first* time. He thus had no 'baggage' or Ego in the ordinary sense, no 'sins', as it were, on his soul, no worldly knowledge, certainly not in the sense in which Zarathustra possessed it. He can thus be regarded as the archetypal Child of Love.

Neither Luke nor Matthew say anything about the childhood of Jesus after his parents settle in Nazareth. Then suddenly he reappears in Luke at the age of 12, i.e. around puberty, just as Luke is about to describe the momentous Temple initiation of Jesus (Luke 2:41-52). Luke tells us it was the practice of Jesus's parents to go to Jerusalem for the Passover every year, and they would bring the boy with them. Such an event was an extended family affair; thus, many people were involved. On the way home, however, after the Passover, the Luke parents become aware that their little boy was missing. He had obviously not set out for home with the larger group. The parents returned hastily to Jerusalem and eventually find their boy in the Temple surrounded by learned doctors and scribes. To their utter astonishment, he is lecturing to the doctors and scribes about scripture and the Law. The boy is transformed! Their beautifully simple child, who up to then had possessed such an aura of innocent, heavenly love that angels came to bless his birth, now suddenly has acquired a wisdom that confounds even the most learned scribes and doctors of the Law. We can see them searching in their dusty old books for confirmation of the words that were pouring from the boy's mouth. He himself, however, needed no books. He spoke directly from his heart. The heart of Love had been filled with Wisdom.

Of all the Gospel accounts of events in the childhood of

Jesus, this is surely the most mysterious. Of course, we cannot know *exactly* what happened to bring this extraordinary change about. Initiation or rebirth by its very nature cannot be described, only experienced. Most adults, however, can come to some understanding of it by simply reflecting on their childhood consciousness and comparing it with their present self-awareness. The inevitable conclusion is this: I am the same person as I was back then, and yet I am totally different! Imagine, then, if such a change were to take place not over twenty, thirty or forty years, but in an instant! Something similar happened in the Temple initiation of the Luke child.

The situation unfolded more or less as follows. The Luke family were not the only ones to come to Jerusalem for the Passover. As many people as possible came. These included the Nathan family and the Solomon Jesus. At a certain propitious moment, both boys were angelically guided out of the crowd and into the inner sanctum of the Temple, the 'Holy of Holies', where it was well known that God spoke directly to the High Priest. While the Luke boy needed little conscious guidance for this to occur, surrounded as he mostly was by angels, seen or unseen, we know that Zarathustra had made long and careful karmic and spiritual preparations for it, preparations admittedly planned often from the spiritual world but carried out through many physical incarnations. It was to be the penultimate act of his great sacrifice to the Sun Spirit, whose most precious human vessel he unquestionably recognised this Child of Love to be. He would, in fact, have long known this. The two children were most likely childhood friends and would have played often together, for both families lived in Nazareth and were connected tribally through their common descent from David.

To this boy, therefore, Zarathustra wished to sacrifice his own physical body. As one of the wisest and most exalted human individualities who ever lived, Zarathustra has the power to incarnate or incorporate his Ego in ways that most of us only dream about. Thus, he was able to vacate his physical body and project, into this Vessel of purest Love, his incarnated spirit-self, or his Ego. The Child of Wisdom, in this miraculous manner, united with the Child of Love, and the individuality we know as Jesus of Nazareth was in effect born.

The description of this important initiation in the life story of Jesus is only given in Luke's Gospel. It stands out rather incongruously in his narrative, somewhat like an unexpected signpost. It seems to be forced into his narrative, as if he felt *obliged* to give it. This otherwise secret event simply *had* to be described, given its importance in relation to the overall Incarnation of the Christ. But no explanation of it is proffered, for that would lead Luke too far down roads of gnosis, of knowledge, and would risk entangling his would-be recipient of the seed-Word of the Gospel in intellectual undergrowths or overgrowths of mind. But being acutely cognisant of the primary importance of faith, it was the *heart* that Luke, and the Evangelists generally, wanted to reach in their Gospel stories.

Luke does, however, give an important hint as to the meaning and importance of this Temple scene. Immediately before *and* after it, he emphasises that his Child of Love is now also to be regarded as being imbued with Wisdom. Before he actually describes the scene, he says: 'The child grew big and strong and full of *wisdom*' (Luke 2:40). And immediately afterwards he repeats: 'As Jesus grew up he advanced in *wisdom* and in favour with God and men' (Luke 2:52).

A full moon node (18 years) is then left out of Luke's version of the life of Jesus of Nazareth, for immediately after the Temple initiation he describes Jesus's final initiation, which is also the first act in the Incarnation of the Christ: the Baptism of Jesus by John in the River Jordan at 30 years of age.

The initiates, and most likely the four canonical Evangelists also, *knew* all these things about Jesus of Nazareth, but from the masses these details were kept back, for 'the sheep' had to be fed only the Word of *faith*. If unprepared persons received the deeper initiation knowledge they were only too likely to mislead both themselves and others, something which did indeed happen, as Paul's Letters in the New Testament well illustrate. This did not auger well for the future of the movement. For as it developed, and as Rome with its in-built hatred of the ancient Mysteries increasingly flexed its muscles within the movement, the intellectual and theological types took over, and the (to us) more interesting and important initiation knowledge was forced completely underground. However, in accordance with a spiritual law whereby knowledge of the spirit cannot ever be extirpated entirely from the world, the Johannine followers of the Rose Cross, that is, the Rosicrucions (and others), kept the initiation tradition alive in Christendom.

The symbol nowadays of this inner spiritual wisdom and knowledge is the Holy Grail. The physical body of the

Nathan or Luke Jesus is thus the fundamental Grail Vessel. The Rosicrucians were primarily responsible for the preservation of this pure Grail wisdom. They knew that soon after Zarathustra vacated his own physical vessel and entered the Grail Vessel of the Luke Jesus, his old Solomon body died, devoid as it was then of its vitalizing principle, the Ego. It was also known that the mother of the Luke child died soon afterwards, as did the father of the Solomon child. The two families then joined together, and this explains why in the Gospels Jesus of Nazareth is sometimes spoken of as having brothers and sisters.

What is known of the life of Jesus of Nazareth during the 18 years between his Temple initiation and his Baptism by John in the River Jordan at the age of 30 is not contained in the canonical Gospels. They are completely silent about it. In Esoteric Christianity, the account of this period is usually called the Fifth Gospel. What is known of it comes either from initiation knowledge or from apocryphal sources. In the canonical Gospels the Baptism takes precedence over everything else. As even a cursory glance at them will show, the Baptism of Jesus is regarded as having the same, or even more importance, than his physical birth.

CHAPTER 7

THE BAPTISM, DEATH, AND RESURRECTION OF JESUS

Most people who call themselves Christians today are not actually Christians at all. They are Jesusians.

The reason for this is that they do not know the difference between Jesus and Christ. This distinction, known in the very early Church, has long been lost to the average believer. Even those who in later times did acquire the knowledge, had to keep silent for fear of persecution, for such knowledge, and gnosis generally, especially from about the 5th century onwards, was deemed heretical by the Church rulers and punishable by excommunication or death. The deeper truth of the Mystery was kept alive, however, but only in secret underground brotherhoods. The established (i.e. Roman) Church wanted no part in this knowledge. To them God was, and still is, Jesus Christ. They don't distinguish between the two. They don't know how. As Jesusians, the Romans first denied and later completely forgot the central and sublime Mystery of Christianity, which is that precisely at the moment Jesus of Nazareth died on the Cross of Golgotha, the Christ was born on Earth.

As recorded in the Gospels, the dead, physical body of Jesus was immediately after his death taken down from the Cross and placed in a tomb. The sun then went dark and a great earthquake occurred. Then on the third day the tomb was found to be empty. The disciples were utterly perplexed as to what had happened. Of course, they would have been aware to varying degrees of the initiation rites, procedures and occurrences of the old Mysteries, for Jesus spoke to them often about these. He was indeed, as the Fifth Gospel records, initiated into many of them in his pre-baptism period, and during that time became more and more aware that it was his own personal destiny to inaugurate a new Mystery on the Earth.

Thus the disciples were undoubtedly expecting *something* to happen when he died. Given all that they had gone through with him, all the amazing things he had done and the wonderful things he had taught them, it was inconceivable that he would simply disappear without trace. He had, of course, prepared them in various ways for the enactment of the new Mystery. Once he even said to them: 'I can pull down the temple of God and rebuild it in three days.' (Matthew 26:61; Mark 14:58; John 2:19). The disciples did not understand what he meant at the time, but he was actually referring to his body. And sure enough, soon after the discovery of the empty tomb, he began to appear to them in his body. But that was quite different. *He* is different at this point. He has a physical body, certainly, as is made crystal clear in the 'down-to-earth' Gospel of Luke, who very pointedly informs us of the Risen One: 'They offered him a piece of fish they had cooked which he took and ate before their eyes' (Luke 24:42). Clearly his *is* a physical body, but one that can appear and disappear at will, a body that can walk through walls and locked doors, etc., as is detailed in the Gospels. For want of a better term, it can be called a physical-spiritual body.

In the old Mysteries it was always the case that after the final initiation of the initiand, a new person was born out of the old one. The new initiate would feel, and absolutely know himself to be, a completely new person. He or she would, however, be aware that their sentient body would still eventually die, in the ordinary physical sense. This indeed was a source of great sadness to them. In the Greek culture especially, physical death was seen as the very essence of tragedy, and the ancient initiates and philosophers always at least *hoped* that this death might somehow be overcome.

With hindsight we can say that they did not hope in vain. For in the new Mystery of the Christ their hopes were actually fulfilled. This Mystery differs from all previous ones in the sense that the person initiated is renewed to such an extent that even his physical body will not die. To put it in reincarnational terms, it will eventually completely overcome death. This is what is called the Resurrection in Christianity. It began on the first Easter Sunday morning when Jesus first appeared to Mary Magdalene outside the tomb. After this he began to appear to people in various places. At length he even appeared to someone who, as a high-ranking Jew, began to legally persecute the followers of Jesus for their stupid and totally blasphemous beliefs. This is Saul of Tarsus, who famously met the Resurrected Jesus on the road to Damascus, and who was so convinced of the living reality of the experience that he changed his name to Paul, abjured his Jewishness and subsequently became, and has remained, one of the Christ's greatest initiates, teachers and ambassadors.

The Resurrection is, of course, a very powerful Mystery. Understandably, those who did not witness it directly had great difficulties with it. It was the same then as now. In the wealthy seaport of Corinth there was a congregation of Christians that Paul himself had established on one of his great missionary journeys after his Damascus initiation. The Corinthians were obviously a very quick-minded people who wanted to know *everything* about the Christ but were given to believe things about him that Paul had not preached. How were they to understand the Resurrection? Their lively questioning actually gave to posterity some of the best available theology on the matter. St Paul probably wrote many letters to the Corinthians. Only two of them, however, are preserved in the *New Testament*. In the first he makes a powerful plea to the Corinthians to believe in the Resurrection. He tells them that at one stage Jesus 'appeared to over five hundred of our brothers at the same time' (1 Cor. 15:6). In the same passage he uses the analogy of a seed to illustrate how the Resurrection is to be understood.

'You may ask, how are the dead raised? In what kind of body? But how foolish! For the seed you sow does not come to life unless it has first died; and what you sow is not the body that shall be, but a naked grain, perhaps of wheat, or of some other kind; and God clothes it with the body of his choice, each seed with its own particular body'
(1 Cor. 15:35-38).

Paul goes on then to talk about the difference between an animal body and a spiritual body and says that Christ is the seed of a new spiritual body for all mankind. Adam, he says, was the first man, but he was a kind of animal-man. Christ, however, is a new kind of man. 'The first man was made "of the dust of the earth"; the second man is from heaven' (1 Cor. 15:46-47). With an uncanny pre-sensing of what many centuries later became the theory of evolution, Paul sees the whole of creation being renewed in and through the sacrificial death and Resurrection of Jesus. In the last book of the New Testament, John's Revelation, John confirms this when he says that Jesus 'is the first-born of the dead' (Rev. 1:5). In other words we can say that by taking the Christ into ourselves we are planting in the soil of our soul the seed of a new sentient body which will, in time, overcome death.

The Resurrection of Christ Jesus is the central mystical fact of the new Mystery of mankind. It is, or certainly was in the past, the key dogma of mainstream Christianity, for the truth of Christ and everything connected with him rests on it. Paul made this as clear as he possibly could when he said in the same passage quoted above: 'If Christ is not raised, then our Gospel is null and void' (1 Cor. 15:14).

Now, the Resurrection of Christ Jesus is intimately linked to his Baptism. You need to understand the significance and meaning of both if you wish to be fully initiated. We said at the beginning of this chapter that upon the death of Jesus, the Christ is born. At the Baptism, however, he is *conceived*. In the cultivation and practice of Esoteric Christianity you need therefore not merely to understand who Jesus is, but also to understand who the Christ is. This requires mental effort, inner spiritual spade-work. Stated in the simplest of terms, Jesus is human, but Christ is divine.

We must turn to John's Gospel in particular if we wish to elucidate the *I Am* spirit of Christ and how this same Spirit was understood in the most ancient scriptures of the world as the universal Self. We saw also how, in the 77th saying of Jesus in the gnostic Gospel Of Thomas, Jesus says of himself, '*I Am* the light that is over all things. *I Am* all. From me all came forth, and to me all extends. Split a piece of wood, and *I Am* there. Lift up a stone and you will find me there.' With these words, Jesus states unequivocally that he is fully in the world. In his *Letter to the Galatians*, Paul expresses this truth most succinctly and clearly when he says that 'Christ is in me.' (Gal. 2:20). He repeats it in his *Letter to the Colossians* where he says to them: 'Christ is in you' (Col. 1:27). Paul, therefore, because of his special initiation, is intimately aware of how Christ is the very Spirit of the Mysteries. Paul is our prime authority for the truth of Esoteric Christianity.

In the ancient pre-Christian Mysteries, however, this Spirit was understood never to fully enter the world in the way that Jesus is indicating in the Gospel Of Thomas, or the way Paul is indicating in his Letters. It was especially the case then that the Spirit did not ever fully enter the human physical body. The experience for the initiate was essentially a mystical one, connected far more with the subtle body, i.e. the etheric/astral body, than the physical body. The Hebrew Prophets, however, pointed to One coming who would make this initiation of the physical body, this awakening to the fullness of the Spirit in the body of flesh and blood, truly possible. This is the Christ. The name is a Hebrew word meaning 'the anointed one', or more correctly in messianic terms, 'the one who is to be anointed,' i.e. Jesus of Nazareth. In gnostic terminology, at his Baptism Jesus is anointed with the 'Fullness of God', which the Gnostics called the Pleroma.

There are many different ways of understanding this initiatory Baptism of Jesus by John, but fundamentally it is through it that the wise Zarathustra individuality of the Matthew Gospel, i.e. Jesus of Nazareth, voluntarily sacrifices or vacates his second physical body, just as he had at 12 years of age vacated his birth body. At that time, as discussed in Chapters 5 and 6, he entered the Nathan Jesus child and soon afterwards his old physical body died. At the Baptism, however, he makes his final and greatest sacrifice to the Sun Spirit, the Logos of the world, whom he had long prophesied would eventually incarnate on the Earth. His spirit Ego now offers up his body to God by vacating Jesus of Nazareth and returning completely to the spiritual world. The Jesus Child of Love of the Luke Gospel, whose body Zarathustra had lived in for a full moon node (18 years), in this way became the anointed Vessel of the ancient prophesies and was filled with the 'Fullness of God'. Because of this he is called the Christ.

Although we all possess a 'spark' of the *I Am* Divinity, Jesus receives its fullness, the Pleroma. He becomes fully One with God. This degree of initiation had never happened in the Mysteries before. Through God entering fully into his physical vessel, Jesus was able to speak of the Divinity and act on its behalf in a way no other person could ever do before. He knew God so intimately he actually calls him Abba, i.e. Father. 'My Father and I are one' (John 10:30).

'Father' is the Christ's name for the great World Spirit. Jesus *knew* his 'Father' to be the Creator Being of the world. This great Being has been known by many names in many religions. His or Its emanations have been seen, imagined and visualized in manifold ways by different peoples all over the world down through the ages. He or It is pictured differently according to a particular culture, its relative development in moral, legal or civic terms, its historical time and geographical place. Very often this visualization takes the form of an animal or a bird.

At the beginning of each of the four Gospels we are told how Jesus is baptized by John. Before this event, however, many people thought John himself was the Messiah. But he wasn't. He was obviously a very powerful spiritual figure, a high Initiate. But precisely because of this he knew himself, and the scriptures, far too well to allow himself to believe, or allow others to believe of him, that he was the Messiah. In a highly significant passage in Luke's Gospel he vehemently denies this: 'I baptise you with water; but there is one to come who is mightier than I. I am not fit to unfasten his shoes. He will baptize you with the Holy Spirit and with fire' (Luke 3:15-17). In each Gospel account of the Baptism, this Spirit is seen by John as a dove. This, no doubt, is due to the type or types of initiations John underwent during his current or former lives. While a bird generally is easily understood as symbolic of spirit *per se*, a dove is a particularly apt manifestation of the Christ Spirit, in that this Spirit is destined to come as close as possible to human beings. Moreover just as the sound a dove makes can sometimes seem like a kind of chatter, at the Baptism its appearance is also accompanied by a voice. In each of the Gospels this is described as a 'voice from heaven' which says of Jesus: 'This is my Son.'

Thus, into the human vessel of Jesus of Nazareth, the World Spirit enters more fully than ever before. There is no better image of the Father than the Son. The early Christians began calling this Spirit holy, for the simple reason that they knew it was divine. For three years after the Baptism, Christ the Son 'sows the seed' of his Father, the Living Word of God, the truth of the Great Spirit, throughout Palestine. For like no other before him he has the power in his Word to awaken the *I Am* in each and every one of his hearers. But the dark Lie, then as now, is loved far more than the shining Truth. The Truth always stirs up fear and hatred. And so Jesus the Christ was crucified. He died on the Cross and his dead body was placed in a tomb by his loving, faithful followers. The sun went dark and a great earthquake occurred. Then on the third day the tomb is found to be empty. What has happened is that over the three years the divine Christ Spirit was slowly but surely permeating the human physical body. Only when the very last cell in that body was fully spiritualized did the body die.

At the same moment the Christ is born. It then took three days for the released cosmic Spirit of the Christ to dissolve and disperse the new archetypal human body into the substance of the Earth, in the ether sphere of which it now lives as an etheric form. There it stands as a living, shining template of the spiritualized form of the human body, a Temple into which all those who take the seed of the Sun-Spirit of Christ into themselves can enter at death and, in an ongoing incarnational, or more correctly, re-incarnational development, eventually become his co-creating brothers and sisters, and in him One with God the Father.

In Christ the forces of Death become the forces of Resurrection, and all who take his Word as the 'Bread of Life' into themselves become part of his universal Body, or the Church, as Paul conceived and theologically formulated it. This, therefore, is the way the divine plan of the world Creator will be fulfilled through the Christ, who becomes the grand Initiator of all mankind.

CHAPTER 8

THE GOSPEL OF JOHN

You should imagine Esoteric Christianity as a glittering, golden crown encrusted with precious, multi-coloured stones. Picture it then on the head of a beautiful young king. Let this king represent the human incarnation of divine Love. Directly above the king's brow, in the centre of the crown, picture one stone bigger than all the others. It is a large white pearl, shining like the sun. In this stone you have a sublime image of the place the Gospel of John has in Esoteric Christianity. It is the jewel in its crown.

In this chapter, we will try to give some indication why this is so.

In the wake of the great incarnational Event that took place in Palestine over 2,000 years ago, a large number of different 'gospels' were written about Christ Jesus. Only four of them, however, gained official recognition by the Roman Church. For this reason, they are called canonical. The rest are, from Rome's (and orthodox Christianity's) point of view, regarded as unreliable, and are therefore called apocryphal. However, given the thoroughgoing Biblical exegesis that has taken place in the last 100 years or so, together with the more recent findings of old and hitherto lost books, especially the Dead Sea Scrolls and the Nag Hammadi Library, the whole concept of 'canonization' has become very outdated.

On the surface, at least, canonization seems like a characteristic power-grab by Rome, a kind of spiritual branding mechanism, the overt purpose of which was to make the Catholic voice loudest within that wonderfully eclectic movement known as The Gnosis, a movement occasioned by the most momentous Event in the spiritual history of mankind, the Incarnation of the Christ.

Rome, however, as history manifestly proves, has done far more to repress true Christianity than uphold it. Today, the historical Church appears to be a fearful, shadowy spectre, representing far more a dreadful devil than a loving God, a doppelganger whose endless machinations work dark and deep down in the psyche of Western humankind, producing nowadays the endless stream of crimes, exploitation and aberrations that fill our news media.

The Irish poet W. B. Yeats saw all this coming a hundred years ago and was inspired to compose one of the best and most famous of his visionary poems, 'The Second Coming', the last lines of which are as follows:

. . . but now I know
That twenty centuries of stony sleep
Were vexed to nightmare by a rocking cradle;
And what rough beast, its hour come round at last,
Slouches toward Bethlehem to be born?

Exorcizing this spectre from the modern soul-consciousness of humankind is the great task of the West. That brave pioneer of our soul-sickness, Sigmund Freud, had already begun it even before Yeats's time; Carl Jung, Freud's more spiritually inclined disciple, took it further along, and the whole process is now in full swing. Anyone with their eyes and ears even half open knows what is going on in the world nowadays: the ever-increasing madness and mayhem, a kind of soul-vomiting necessary, in a twisted way, to its ultimate healing.

Yeats was an esoteric Christian. Many of his poems, and indeed his life story itself, tell us clearly that he was instinctively aware of the need for a spiritual revolution which would transform the old, tired and much distorted countenance of Christ. That time is now at hand. A new Christian consciousness, visionary and cosmic in nature, is germinating beneath the polluted surface of our world, and in our even more polluted minds. It is a vision based on a knowledge and a truth that was very much alive in early Christianity but has been all but lost, and consequently must be called esoteric.

It is the hidden wisdom of our planet's God, and it is spoken of very powerfully and revealingly by St. Paul in his Letter to the Colossians in the New Testament. It is also unquestionably the foundation stone of all Paul's teaching there, which he summed up in his revolutionary utterance: 'Christ is in you' (Col. 1:27). Elsewhere in his Letters, Paul speaks of this as God's open secret, revealed by and through the Christ. It is the original, revolutionary, and ecstatic truth of real Christianity which all Christ's followers discover. The secret can therefore be thought of and stated thus: Christ is in me; through him I will overcome all pain, suffering and death, and gain eternal life.

This is this open secret of the first Christians, which is based on the gnosis of self-knowledge. It is also what the Romans hated most. For bestowing as it does on each individual who has faith in Christ the knowledge that he or she is a god in the making, a being possessing the glorious hope of a truly divine and eternal freedom, it vitiates the power and authority of all external entities, whether these be elemental, cosmic, religious or political.

Thus, especially from the time that Constantine lifted his Edict against the Christians (313 AD) and began his politically cunning campaign of subsuming these 'holy ones' into the decaying organism of his empire in order to resurrect it, the Gnostics became a thorn in the side of the ecclesia. Constantine ensured that this latter entity was redirected and refashioned into a purely Roman one which was then to become the ultimate authority in *all* matters, spiritual or social, political or religious. Henceforth anything to do with self-knowledge or a self-regulating, inner authority would be considered heretical. Gnosis, in other words, went completely against Rome's programme for a universal, monotheistic, monolithic, centrally controlled world religion.

The Romans succeeded in this enterprise not only

because they built on the back of the Christ's Great Sacrifice, but by resuscitating the political dregs of their all but dead imperium. Copying a new legal system, Canon Law, from the labyrinth of the Jewish Torah, they created a kind of machine which first usurped then deadened the thriving bio-etheric power of the essentially human organism that the ecclesia, the 'body of Christ' (the Church), possessed up to this.

Paul knew the bio-ether power of Christ's body intimately. Through his powerful Damascus initiation, he became aware that the Risen One had brought something entirely new to the spiritual life of mankind. He became absolutely imbued with the Christ. Formerly he was a fanatical Jew. Now he poured all his zeal into proclaiming the new God. To hell, he said, with imperialism, nationalism and especially all that old, dusty, forbidding Law of Jehovah. There is a new Faith and a new God; and because of this there is also a new kind of Justice. It is cosmic, and it comes from Christ. In him there is a fully atoned, sin-free, sun-life now to be had. This is pure Christ-consciousness.

Paul is the greatest of the Gnostics. In fact, all Paul's Letters in the New Testament should be read carefully by anyone genuinely interested in practising Esoteric Christianity. The open-hearted study of these texts, properly translated, can actually become a form of Christian initiation. However, it is to John's Gospel, studded with its wonderful *I Am* sayings of Jesus, to which you must turn for the fullest elaboration of the fundamental but mystical truth of the Christ revelation. Despite all the recent unearthing of lost manuscripts and the resulting scholarly exegesis which is giving rise to far-reaching changes in

Christian consciousness, the canonical Gospel of John remains outstanding when it comes to the elaboration of the truths of Christ. Thus, insofar as our time urgently calls for a reappraisal and even reinvention of the original Gnosis, John's Gospel can truly be called gnostic.

Even the early 'canonizers' had difficulty with it in this regard. They hated the Gnostics, yet this document by John they simply could not ignore, for it contained information and knowledge that every Christian, Gnostic or otherwise, should have. Fully realizing that it was a text with a unique style, content and ability to convince, they felt duty-bound to include it in their canon for fear that it might get lost to posterity. For this reason, of the four canonical Gospels, to use a rather crude and hackneyed metaphor, it sticks out like a sore thumb. For this reason also, scholars describe the first three Gospels as synoptic, meaning they share a general or common view of Jesus and his life. These read, however, like a piecing together into a more or less coherent story of various sayings of Jesus and known events in his life. Documentation of such sayings were inevitably extant in the years immediately after Jesus died. John's Gospel, on the other hand, reads like it is written by someone who knew Jesus not only personally but very intimately. This intimacy allows John to depict the figure of Jesus with far more reverence and majesty than the synoptic writers, or indeed the writers of any of the other Gospels. Thus, John's is the Gospel *par excellence* for spiritual study and meditation, for our souls change fundamentally when, with reverence, we allow the figure depicted therein to work on us. The mystical Christ comes alive within us when we meditate on John's Gospel. This is why we call it the crown in the jewel of Esoteric Christianity.

The opening words of this most remarkable and unique book are justifiably world famous: 'In the beginning was the Word.' John wrote in Greek. Thus his 'word' must be capitalized in English because it is a direct translation of the supremely definitive Greek word 'logos' which John uses to characterize the divinely creative being or spirit of God at work in the world, specifically the Christ.

Before his 'baptism', John was probably a pupil of the Greek Mysteries at the Temple of Diana in Ephesus. It is known that he also ended his life in that city. In the Temple there, the central Mystery teaching was concerned with the spoken word. It was taught there that the human being is a micro-logos and the universe a macro-logos, and that only by understanding one could the other be understood. John thus sees the Christ in cosmic terms and regards him as the incarnated Logos, or the 'Word made flesh' (John 1:14). As a convert from the ancient Mysteries to the new Way of the Christ, John would have been fully aware of how, in the wake of the Great Sacrifice of the Christ, a new scriptural testimony of God was needed in the world to replace the old Hebrew one.

A close study of John's book reveals a remarkably careful composition. He begins by rewriting the opening passage of the Hebrew Bible in the Book of Genesis, and boldly identifies the world-creating Elohim, written of there, with the Logos. Then, also in accord with the opening of Genesis, he further identifies the Logos as the 'light of the world'. But a little further on he makes his grand and unique assertion: 'And the Word became flesh' (John 1:14). He goes on to give an account, often astonishingly precise in detail, of the teaching and miraculous events of the life of his beloved Master and ends his book with a statement that is a perfect counterpoise to his opening one: 'There is much else that Jesus did, but if it were all to be recorded in detail, I suppose the whole world could not hold the books that would have to be written' (John 21:25).

John has, in other words, the clearest possible vision of Christ in that he sees in him, in his very flesh and blood, what the Gnostics called the Pleroma, or the absolute fullness of God. Only someone who knew the Master very intimately could have written about him in this way. John speaks often in his book about the beloved disciple of Jesus, and precisely because of the spiritually intimate nature of his revelations about the Master, John adopts a curious narrative style which allows him only towards the end of the book to reveal the beloved disciple to be himself.

It is the very nature of this intimacy that allows John to act as a guide to all those who seek the Christ, not through the path of an outdated religiosity, but inwardly through a conscientiously practised self and soul development. John actually *knows* while all others are still seeking. His Gospel illustrates this perfectly when it is to him all the other disciples turn when they want to know who Jesus means when he says, 'One of you will betray me' (John 13:21).

If, then, the Gospel is the Living Word, John's is more alive than any. He alone the capacity to come alive *himself* for the sincere soul who 'eats' his words, that is, for the one who deeply meditates his Gospel. He knows this very well and in fact writes about it at the end of his book, where he describes the sublime early morning meal by the sea with the resurrected Jesus. There Peter enquires of Jesus what will happen to the Beloved Disciple (i.e. John), and Jesus clearly indicates that he will remain alive until he, Jesus himself, returns again, that is, until his Second Coming (John 21:22).

Why does John cause Jesus to speak so prophetically about him? What gives John such unique authority? And what made the early 'canonizers' realize that, despite its obvious gnostic overtones, this book of John's simply *had* to be passed on to future generations?

Was it the overall nature of this Gospel, the unique if highly individualized insight that John imparts there into the being of the Christ, or was there something more to it? Did in fact the 'canonizers' know some secret about John, something that was so extraordinary and revolutionary that John could not even write about it himself? There was, and it is this: John is Lazarus, the one that Jesus raises from the dead in the last of the seven great miracles he performed, as recounted by John in his Gospel.

The great Christian initiate of the last century, Rudolf Steiner, revealed this occult secret to all modern spiritual seekers, writers and researchers. It is the key piece of spiritual knowledge that clears up all the confusion regarding the relationship of Lazarus to John, of John to the Beloved Disciple, and of how all this relates to the writer of the fourth Gospel.

It was the Beloved Disciple that Christ publicly raised from the dead in the greatest of his miracles (the greatest, that is, apart from his own Resurrection). Through this miracle, Jesus wished to demonstrate on the one hand that he himself was part of an ancient Mystery tradition and that he could only be fully understood in that light; on the other hand, he was categorically demonstrating that he was inaugurating a great new Mystery (see Chapter 4).

The purpose of the old Mysteries always was to awaken in the neophyte the knowledge that there lived in him or her a divine spark of the spirit of God. After many years of training and preparation, the neophyte was finally put into a death sleep and when awoken by the hierophant was reborn with the tremendous realization that the Logos now lived in him and that he was truly a Son of God. In this way the pupil became an initiate and could speak the Word of God's Mystery in the world at large.

Lazarus, as Jesus's closest and most loved disciple, would have been taught all these things by Jesus before he, Lazarus, passed away. Jesus could of course have healed Lazarus before he died, but John's unique position in the constellation of Jesus's closest disciples actually meant that Jesus *had to* let him die, for Jesus needed to use this death to perform his greatest miracle. Through Lazarus, Jesus accomplishes the great transmutation of life in the sense of the ancient Mysteries. At his awakening, Lazarus naturally becomes aware of this and inevitably sees Jesus himself as an incarnated Mystery. He clearly saw in Jesus the living fulfilment of *all* the hidden Mysteries of old, an actual *personification* of the immemorial tradition of the Mysteries. Jesus therefore is for Lazarus the 'Living Word', the 'Word made Flesh', and from then on, the Grand Initiator of all humankind.

Initiates in the Mysteries always received a new name

at their awakening. Lazarus took one of the most profound of the ancient Mystery names: Ioannes. It is a name which echoes the primordial wisdom and power of God, the oceanic sound of his creative voice. The book which John later wrote about this Living Word, i.e. his Gospel, reflects this. It is a unique book in that it is the only one to have been written by someone who came back from the dead. It is literally a biography of God, and its meditation has the power to awaken the human soul to its own majesty and grandeur in that it awakens the Christ within.

When John tells us that Jesus said that he (John) might not die in the ordinary sense, (John 21-23) he is indirectly indicating a doctrine that was, at the time he wrote the book, anathema to both the Jews and the Romans alike: reincarnation. As his other great book in the New Testament, The Apocalypse, shows, he was clairvoyantly aware of all the Powers, whether psychic, spiritual or physical, that would oppose the Christ in the world, and would try their best to repress the truth of his great New Mystery. John was hinting, therefore, in his beautiful description at the end of his book of the morning meal by the sea, that he himself would stay very close to human beings in the future and even physically incarnate as much as possible. It was a kind of Gospel pledge he made then to keep the Christ Truth alive in an ever-darkening world.

John succeeded admirably in this. Esotericists and occultists have long known that John has had many incarnations since the 1st century. Currently the best known of these is as Christian Rosenkreutz in the 13th and 14th centuries, and in the 18th century as the Count Saint

Germain. However, whether he is incarnated in a physical body or not, through his Gospel primarily, but also in many other esoteric ways, he continues to exert a powerful influence on all who genuinely strive to live as true Christians.

CHAPTER 9

MEDITATION

I t almost goes without saying that if you genuinely and sincerely desire knowledge of the Christ, in the initiatory sense outlined in the preceding chapters, you will need to work at it. This primarily means meditation.

In Chapter 6 I described how in very early Christianity both knowledge (gnosis) of and faith (belief) in the Christ was cultivated. As Christianity developed, however, especially under the tutelage of old, decaying and imperial Rome, the gnostic or knowledge aspect of the movement was suppressed, and the faith aspect only was promulgated. This led to theology eventually taking the place of philosophy, and dogma and doctrine taking the place of individual spiritual enquiry. From the time of Rome's dominance of Christianity onward, you were not allowed to find you own way to Christ. You had, under the pain and threat of eternal punishment, to follow the direction of a priest, your bishop, the pope etc. You were simply forced to pray, to go to church and so on. That was the technique adopted and the methodology used in the spreading of Christianity after the defeat of the gnostic church. From about the 4th or 5th century onwards, Rome intended the Christian Way to become nothing less than a centrally organized, universal, *mass* religion.

It was because of Rome's one-sided and very militaristic approach to the humble Christian Way that meditation as a form of spiritual practice and development was viewed by Rome with great suspicion. For Rome correctly associated meditation with knowledge and prayer with faith, and thus promulgated the latter only. Meditation, however, as a form of spiritual discipline as distinct from prayer, had been cultivated in the East for millennia prior to Christianity. It also played an important part in the various mystery and gnostic schools that comprised the essential core of the early, pre-Roman, Christian movement.

The suppression of Gnosticism by the Roman Church went hand-in-hand with the suppression of the great and ancient art, one could say even the spiritual *science*, of meditation. Esoteric Christianity kept it alive, however, albeit secretly, and in doing so also kept alive the essential knowledge aspect of the Christ mystery in Europe in the dark age of Christianity. This dark age is now thankfully over, and the time is ripe for meditation to make a general comeback in Christianity. I would go so far as to say that the entire future of true Christianity depends on people taking up the art and practice of meditation.

The reason I say this is that nowadays *knowledge of* Christ must be put on an equal footing with *faith in* him. This is not in any way to disparage the practice of faith or of prayer. The Church was able to impose faith on the masses in the past because generally speaking it was felt that Christ could not be fully known or truly understood. People were told and taught to *believe* in him, certainly. But *knowledge* of him was (correctly!) deemed to be something different. The old Roman Church dictum was: Believe that you may know. Back then it was considered that ordinary human thinking could not grasp the deep, cosmic meaning and universal truth of the Christ. But human thinking has developed greatly in the two millennia since the advent of Christ, precisely through the vitalizing influence of Christianity on the mind and psyche of the masses. The average modern human being has a much greater self-awareness than was the case in the first centuries of our era. Our consciousness is quite different from that of the ancients. The progress of civilization is also the progress and development of consciousness itself. They go hand-in-hand. And the essential difference between now and way back then is due undoubtedly to the influence of *science*.

The progress of science in the last few hundred years is astonishing. The result is that the consciousness of the average person nowadays is *scientistic* in nature. People are no longer content to simply believe what they are told. They want to know why they should believe. This applies to everything, but most especially to religion and the spiritual life, which explains the rise in popularity of movements such as scientology. Thus, whereas faith may have been sufficient in the past as an expression of belief in Christ, for the average modern person, faith, if they have it at all, merely creates an appetite for spiritual knowledge which orthodox Christianity, by virtue of its whole history from the 5th century onwards, cannot satisfy.

This dire situation accounts, I believe, for the pandemic of mental illness in our time. The failure of established religion to provide real spiritual nourishment creates a hole in the soul and psyche of the average person, a hole that ultimately can only be filled with the Bread of Life, i.e. knowledge of the living Christ. The new dictum of Christianity therefore should be the reverse of the old one: Know that you may believe.

Now, the knowledge of Christ that I give in this book and elsewhere, and which is the basis of Esoteric Christianity, comes through the practice of meditation. Thus, all the words that I write about Esoteric Christianity here and elsewhere merely point you in the direction of an experience which you can gain in your own unique way. This knowledge, which applies to almost everyone on planet Earth, is summed up in the Pauline words: 'Christ is in you.' (Col. 1:27) It is an initiation or rebirth experience, an inner Christ baptism that was the core objective and vital force in early Christianity, and which it is the task of Esoteric Christianity to promote and cultivate in the modern world. Through the practice of Christ-conscious meditation, this, the true baptism, inevitably comes about.

I cannot go into the art, theory and practice of meditation more deeply here, except to say that if you do not already meditate, or even if you do and you wish to reorient your spiritual life along the lines of Esoteric Christianity as outlined here, then the Gospel of John is highly recommended as a source of meditation material. The short but profound Prologue to this Gospel can be meditated with ever increasing spiritual enlightenment by anyone with an open mind and heart. The several *I Am* sayings of Jesus in this Gospel are also wonderful subjects for meditation, as indeed are any of the healings, parables and scenes in the life of Jesus.

The one thing I would say about meditation generally is that its true value, its lasting and best results come from the pure and persistent practice of it more than anything else, in other words, from the *discipline* of it. Thus, the content of meditation must always take second place to the discipline of the practice of meditation generally. The word 'discipline' is derived from 'disciple', and only through the daily and dedicated practice of meditation does a modern person become a true disciple of the spirit in the age-old sense.

CHAPTER 10

THE HOLY GRAIL

Esoteric Christianity can also be called Grail Christianity. There are many reasons for this but the fundamental one is that after the Church abandoned the core esoteric truth of Christ, and indeed made the pursuit of such an inner way to him heretical, those who endeavoured to keep this way open and this spirit alive in the West, found in the object of the Holy Grail the perfect image for their great work.

It is not our intention to go into detail here about the history of the Grail, the Grail movement or the meaning and elite purpose of the Grail Family etc. There is an extensive literature on these matters, much of which, alas, is of a spurious nature, for the Grail tends to over-excite the weak imagination of intellectuals, as well as stimulating a passion for making easy money. It is sufficient for our purposes here to understand the Grail as the Cup or Chalice Jesus used at the Last Supper, and in which Joseph of Aramathea collected some of Jesus's Blood when he was taken down dead from the Cross the following day. This Object then became, and remains, an extant, very powerful, albeit concealed, relic of Jesus. For the Rosicrucians, the Cathars, the Templars and many other lesser known groups, it became a means of focussing, organizing, channelling and deepening their work on the inner path to Christ. Such people in the Middle Ages constituted a kind of invisible counter Church. Thus, whereas the orthodox or mainstream Church became at this time a dark, repressive institution whose method was terror and whose agents dealt in cruelty, death and genocide, the Holy Grail became a bright counter-focus for pure Christian hope, love and faith. The faith of the Grail seekers was not based on the dogmatic and enforced belief of the ever more power-seeking Roman Catholic Church, however, but on a deep love of, and commitment to, the true inner Christ.

The soft, blood-filled vessel of the heart responds to the sublime reality of this spiritual Being far more than the hard, bony head. The faculty of *feeling*, therefore, needs not only to be enriched and enlivened but *purified* if we are to properly approach the matter of the Grail and partake of its contents.

The life of feeling is purified primarily through beauty, art and the creative imagination. We have shown in Chapter 3 how the Church fears imagination. There is good reason for this, for although the imagination is the creator of much good, it is also an arch-creator of false hope, superficial joy and real fear. Left to itself it grows wild and often leads people astray from truth and knowledge; the imagination needs, in other words, to be *educated*. When this is properly done – and it is done best through the cultivation and practice of Esoteric Christianity – it leads to a higher kind of knowledge than that gained through Church theology, general philosophy or the intellect alone. It leads, in fact, to true spiritual knowledge.

First, however, it must be acknowledged that the human imagination is very mysterious. How, for instance, do you distinguish it from consciousness, or from feeling, or indeed especially from thinking itself? Actually, in earlier, pre-Socratic times, imagination was an important part of thinking. In the West, however, especially through the influence of Greek philosophy, thinking became progressively more rational, scientific and abstract, so that in our modern, post-Enlightenment culture, thinking has become very machine-like or mechanical, and utterly devoid of feeling.

The mainstream Church is largely responsible for this state of affairs in that through its fear of the imagination it abandoned the true spirit of Christ, and in the process sacrificed its traditional moral power and authority to the pseudo-religion of materialistic science. And the hypnotic fascination with technology that this science then produced has so alienated humankind from their home – Mother Earth – that they have all but forgotten their true spirit-endowed origin, and as a result have unwittingly manufactured an ecological catastrophe of apocalyptic dimensions. Moreover, this tragedy will never either be properly addressed, or the damage redressed, unless human beings clearly acknowledge that the world is as magical as it is mechanical. The practitioners of Esoteric Christianity have a great responsibility in this regard in that they are, as it were, 'a chosen few' who make a genuine start on this very long road to redemption.

Therefore we say that by placing the Grail at the centre of our meditations we have the perfect image to evoke the magical universe. However, for most people the inherited mechanical mode of thinking is a huge barrier to making progress. In this regard the first thing you have to do, therefore, is to change you thinking habits. The Grail helps enormously in this inner work because through it you learn to enliven your thinking with the warmth of human feeling and the creative power of your imagination.

There are many ways of cultivating this 'Grail thinking' but a fundamental one is the practice of meditation, as indicated in the previous chapter. Practised within the context of Esoteric Christianity, meditation and concentration strengthen ordinary thinking, but in a magical rather than a mechanical way. Indeed, sincere and dedicated practitioners will find that by enlivening their thinking they will be able to penetrate the material world and its objects and reveal to their awakened Ego the spiritual reality that underlies *all* existence. This, in fact, is the initiation that Esoteric Christianity promises to the sincere practitioner. Through it, imagination in the ordinary sense is raised to a higher or purely cognitive level whereby experiences of spiritual Beings and events are vouchsafed that are as real as any of, or in, the purely material work-a-day world. Similarly, just as for ordinary mechanical thinking the Holy Grail can become an object of intellectual fascination, for the enlivened thinking of the meditator it becomes a focus for the magical universe and in this sense acquires a more and more real aspect.

Thus, as you educate your imagination in accordance with the principles and truths of Esoteric Christianity, you not only learn to think differently, but to *see* differently, for living thinking is to mechanical thinking as the taste of an orange is to merely seeing it. You learn, in other words, to *live into* things and not merely see them. You learn, in fact, to *see through* them. Words and concepts become less fixed and more mobile. You become more and more conscious and feel more and more the *living reality* not just of our Mother Earth but of the entire cosmos and its manifold Beings.

This experience is essentially an expansion, a deepening, and most importantly a *purifying* of your blood. You live in your blood. Blood is, in fact, the *life* of all animals and human beings, and the most important thing to remember is that your Ego, that is, your pure spiritual, higher Self, lives in your blood. Your blood is the vessel of your spirit Self. That is the essential Grail secret.

Because the Holy Grail can become for you, as a sincere meditator, the magically real Vessel that contains the Blood of the Christ, it can also become that through which the deepest and most intimate understanding of him is made possible. For to know the Grail is to drink from it, and to drink from it is to drink the quintessential magical substance of life. The Grail, therefore, is the object of purest devotion, of truest and holiest communion with Christ, offering you, as a gift, the transformational substance of pure spiritual consummation. This truth is confirmed in the sublime Gospel of John when Jesus says that whoever 'drinks my blood dwells in me and I in him' (John 6:56).

CHAPTER 11

THE REAPPEARANCE
OF CHRIST

In addition to his Gospel recounting the life and teachings of Jesus, St. Luke also wrote one of the other main books of the New Testament. It is called The Acts of the Apostles, or more often simply (The) Acts. Luke opens it with an account of the Resurrection and how for forty days the Risen One appeared to various people. Then Luke says that this Jesus gathered some of his closest disciples around him, brought them to a mountain and spoke his final words before disappearing altogether, an event known as the Ascension. The disciples, acutely aware of how tiny a group they were, despite bearing witness to the greatest Event of all time, enquired of their departing Lord when his rulership of the Earth would be fulfilled. However, he seemed to brush off their query as naivety. 'It is not for you to know about dates and times,' he replied. 'These are under the control of my Father' (Acts 1:7). After offering his disciples a few words of comfort and encouragement, Luke says that Jesus 'was lifted up and a cloud removed him from their sight' (Acts 1:9).

With great sadness the disciples looked up for a long time at the sky. Suddenly two angels appeared and said, 'Men of Galilee, why stand there looking up into the sky? This Jesus, who has been taken away from you up to heaven, will come again in the same way as you have seen him go' (Acts 1:11).

Thus, the early Christians eagerly awaited this return of the Christ, which they believed to be imminent, as is evident from many other verses in the New Testament. But although in the two millennia that have elapsed since his disappearance many have claimed to be him (as he himself predicted in Matthew 24:5, etc.), he has not returned. This is best explained by a close reading of this present book, which, though it emphasizes both the historicity and physical reality of the Christ, places primary emphasis on an *inner* relationship to him. And while this inner experience can be more fulfilling than any of the outer material world, it nevertheless has its roots in, and grows out of, that world. . This is the sense in which Jesus speaks in the earlier quoted logia from the gnostic Gospel of Thomas: '*I Am* the light that is over all things. *I Am* all. From me all came forth, and to me all extends. Split a piece of wood, and *I Am* there. Lift up a stone and you will find me there.'

Although the Christian Gnostics did not disparage faith as such, they were concerned not with a simplified, half-pagan Jesus faith, but with a Christ-centred schooling of the mind. They were aware of the holy spiritual Presence of the Christ even though he had vanished from physical sight. But precisely because of this they knew they had to learn to see him in a new way, in a new, poetic or world-creative light.

This new way of Christian seeing is summed up very beautifully in the following poem by the Irish poet Joseph Mary Plunkett (1887-1916):

I SEE HIS BLOOD UPON THE ROSE

I see his blood upon the rose
And in the stars the glory of his eyes,
His body gleams amid eternal snows,
His tears fall from the skies.

I see his face in every flower;
The thunder and the singing of the birds
Are but his voice – and carven by his power
Rocks are his written words.

All pathways by his feet are worn,
His strong heart stirs the ever-beating sea,
His crown of thorns is twined with every thorn,
His cross is every tree.

When the Gospel reached illiterate Ireland in the 5th century, it was not received intellectually, as was the case in the original field of its evangelization, the decadent Roman Empire. Because Ireland was never touched by literacy, by the imperium of Rome or indeed the culture of Greece, it received the Gospel primarily through the Grail vessel of the heart. This produced in Ireland an altogether different kind of Christianity than that which had developed in the four and a half centuries since its inception in Palestine, i.e. the intellectual, cerebral or dogmatic form of Christianity that was spearheaded by Rome. In Ireland the Gospel story appealed far more to the imagination than the brain, to the heart more than the head, and this in turn gave rise to what may be called the Golden Age of Christianity, i.e. the Celtic Church of the 6th and 7th centuries. As the poem above and many other aspects of Irish culture clearly show, this Christ-centred sensitivity to Mother Earth has remained strong and vibrant in Ireland, even right up to modern times, and having incarnated in the southern part of the country, I am privileged to share in it.

Of course, seeing and sensing the planet as a living Being did not originate with the early Christians. The ancients before them saw living, spiritual Beings and forces in almost everything, in the trees, the rivers and the clouds, that is, in Nature generally. This way of seeing and understanding the world is called pantheism, Pan being the Greek god of Nature. But when at the Last Supper Christ took bread and wine and said that from now on human beings should regard these substances as *his* body and *his* blood, he was initiating something unique, extra-ordinary and absolutely revolutionary in the life of humankind. At his Baptism he had already fully committed himself to a sacrificial death. It was not until the Last Supper, however, that the full import and meaning of this flooded like a cosmic dam-burst into his consciousness. He knew then that by offering himself freely as a sacrificial victim for the atonement of mankind's constant sinning, he was consciously replacing animal blood, which up to this had constituted the offering, with human blood. Moreover, by replacing the sacrificial altar of the Temple with the Earth itself he was endowing all future spiritual thinking with a purely monistic impulse, enabling all generations following him to see the One God living, weaving and working in all things, but most especially in the fruits of the Earth.

When thinking becomes Christianised in this way, especially through the practice of Esoteric Christianity, it also quickens in the practitioner the development of the newly emerging cognitive organ referred to earlier (see Chapter 3). This, which may be called the Grail organ, allows the warm blood of the feeling heart far more access to the cold functioning of the brain-bound intellect, and results in a higher form of cognition, a new and essentially clairvoyant mode of seeing.

This new way of seeing brings to the practitioner many new feelings of hope and joy. But for these to be *pure*, meaning not coloured by egotistic, animalistic or lower impulses, they must be accompanied in the practitioner by a clear understanding that he or she is in possession not only of an outer physical body comprising the substance of flesh and blood, but also of an inner body comprising the substance of pure light, thought and memory.

In the religious practises and spiritual schools of the East, for millennia prior to Christianity, knowledge of this body was cultivated. It was given various names, including the subtle body, the mental body, the life-force body, the time body or even the memory body, and an extensive teaching and literature existed, and still exists, about it. The Gnostics also cultivated this knowledge, albeit in their own way, while in the elite Hebrew Mysteries the subtle body was assigned to the sphere of *Yesod*, one of the lower sephiroth on the cabbalistic Tree of Life. The appearance on Earth of the enigmatic Christ body, however, meant that this knowledge had to undergo a complete revision and update. For back then everyone who came into contact with the Christ Event and who had even the slightest interest in spiritual matters knew that this Christ had brought something entirely new into *all* aspects of life on Earth. A new way of thinking was now required for acquiring true knowledge of *everything*, whether in the Earth below or the cosmos above, of *all* bodies, forms and figures.

This was the great challenge that the Christian Gnostics undertook: how to see Christ Jesus in the *correct light*. They worked at it heroically, but from our perspective they were severely handicapped, for they had no real understanding of light, and thus also of time. Herein lies the problem of the return of Christ. When? While admittedly time remains a mystery, we can certainly speak and think of it in a more realistic way than our ancient forbears. For even an ordinary schoolboy or girl today will know what is meant by light-years. Such a concept would have meant nothing to the ancients, however. They had an altogether different, we would say simpler, understanding of time and space, of dates, and indeed of history generally. However, the two millennia that have passed since the disappearance of Christ have given *us* a perspective on these matters undreamt of by the early Christians. And from the perspective of Esoteric Christianity, we can begin to truly understand the mystery of time, and by extension the return of Christ, only through the subtle body, not through the intellect alone.

Our first contact with the Gospel is, of course, through the brain-bound intellect. The seed Word of God was traditionally, and still is, to some degree at least, sown there. It should be realized, however, that for this seed to *germinate*, that is, for it to break its skin, transform, grow and ultimately flourish in the Christian sense, it needs a certain type of 'soil'. And while it may be true that in the past the cold, hard 'stuff' of the brain-bound intellect provided this 'soil' for the spread of Christendom and the growth of the Church, it must also be admitted that this growth is today rapidly withering away. Anyone with even a modicum of genuine spiritual sensitivity knows and feels this. The cold stone Church of the past has served its purpose, whatever it was. Its day is done! We urgently need a new Church. But for it to survive the ever-growing presence and power of Evil in the world, it must be built with an altogether different kind of stuff than the intellect provides.

The Christian intellect in its pristine form, i.e. that of the first disciples, most notably Paul, was light-filled, love-filled, majestic and magically powerful. However, as Christ himself predicted, his name and power would be usurped by various human and cosmic forces opposed to him and to God. See what has happened: the Christian intellect was first muddied, then dreadfully deformed by the decadent, covetous and corrupting power of Roman ideology. This gave rise more recently to the centuries of materialism. All of this has led us to our present apocalyptic demise. Tampering with carbon or atoms, however, merely treats the symptoms of our planetary illness. We must get to the root cause. The collapse is coming. If we are to be saved from mass extinction we urgently need to build a new image, form a new healing relationship with the Planetary Ruler, our Christ. The irony is that while we have to learn to experience him in a new light, through a new kind of thinking and seeing other than the abstract intellect, it is nevertheless also the way in which the first Christians saw him, that is, through his life-body.

In Esoteric Christianity this subtle body is called the etheric body, and today's true Christians must get to know it and the cosmic stuff it is made of in order to partake of their allotted share of the Christ Body. In other words, they must learn to see and feel, to *be* in the world in a new way. Fundamentally our world will not be saved through inter-governmental treaties, economic programmes and such like (although these can help), but through the strength of individual, free and wilful moral effort. Each one of us needs to use our time and effort fundamentally to build our own house of Christ, our own 'interior castle'. This, of course, is also the 'house with many mansions' where Jesus says he prepares a place for everyone who faithfully follows him (John 14:2). The 'stuff' of this house is also the 'stuff' of our life-body, the Earth's ether, which pours in constantly from the cosmos. Its cultivated entry into our *self*-consciousness cures miraculously, for in its essence it is spiritual, holy and healing. You can understand, therefore, how our planet Earth, having received into it the atoning, sacrificial Blood of the cosmic Christ over two thousand years ago, is now fully permeated by this divine substance and consequently by the ether of Christ's body.

When, in John's Gospel, Christ says '*I Am* the Bread of Life', he is referring directly to this mystery of life on Earth. He is saying that this life differs *fundamentally* from matter. Of course, an intellectually proud modern scientist may try to prove to you that there is no absolute difference, in material terms, between, say, a stone and a lion; but if he fails to convince you, it is probably because you have more common sense than he!

For there *is* a difference, and it *is* absolute: it is that the lion has a life-body and the stone does not. In order for something to have life, it must have a life-body. The life-body gives force and form to all living things. As already stated, in the East this body was often called the mental body, but this was precisely because, through the sustained practice of meditation as was common in the East, they understood and clearly experienced the Logos or formative power of *pure thinking*.

Modern, abstract, scientific thinking denies this absolute nature of life. Modern scientific thinking is a dead form of thinking because it insists on using the same concepts for living forms as for dead ones. But to understand what life really is requires a different kind of thinking, a living, mobile, picture thinking. Ultimately this kind of thinking is clairvoyant, visionary and often prophetic in nature. It is the kind of thinking that the Master Jesus teaches. '*I Am* the Way, the Truth and the Life' (John 14:6). The beloved disciple, John, absorbed into the fullness of his being this new Way, and it was the new kind of thinking it produced that enabled him to write not only his sublime Gospel, but also his *Apocalypse*, the last book of the New Testament. At the very end of this great book of visions John declares, 'He who gives this testimony speaks: "Yes, *I Am* coming soon."'

For those who can open their hearts to the Christ, this time is at hand! We live at a crucial moment in the history of the world. It is important to remember, however, that this return of Christ cannot be in an individualized *physical* body as you currently know this. He appeared once in such a form and died. This Christ Event was a once only happening in the history not only of humanity, but of the entire cosmos. The Christ is a cosmic Being. He descended from higher worlds to a single, unique Incarnation, following which he would never again enter a physical body. The body that arose from the grave was not, therefore, an ordinary physical body, but an etherized one, visible only to etheric vision, after the manner described above.

With the reappearance of Christ in the spiritual, bio-etheric world which borders on the material world of the physical senses, a whole new phase of Christianity begins. This is decidedly *not* a renewal of the old Church or of Christianity generally, but a completely new developmental phase of the original Christ impulse, which has relevance for the whole of the Earth and the universe and for all time to come. 'Heaven and earth shall pass away, but my words shall not pass away.' (Matthew 24:35)

This new development in Christianity is based on a knowledge and a vision of the Christ that was initially cultivated alongside faith and belief in him. This can be verified by surviving gnostic texts but more importantly by the canonical *Letters* of Paul in the New Testament.

However, the visionary or mystical aspect of the new Way was suppressed because in its individualized nature it could not be formulated into language that could be generally understood. All of this also meant, of course, that it severely clashed with the Roman-inspired programme for a worldwide, catholic faith or orthodox religion based on the Christ.

However, explaining the fact that knowledge and vision of Christ seemed to many of these early Christians to transcend human logic and thinking did not by any means stop people thinking about Christ. This thinking in fact went on and reached its culmination in the 19th century, especially in the German Idealist philosophers, who indeed may be said to have cleared the way for the reappearance of Christ in the 20th century. It is only idealist thinking which makes it possible for the original vision and knowledge of Christ to be fully understood by modern people.

At the beginning of the 20th century something came to pass that had long been prophesied in the Eastern religions. It was the ending of the Kali Yuga, or the Age of Darkness. A New Age of light then began to dawn. The horrible happenings of the 20th century were but the shadow that this new light cast, for always the brighter the light, the darker the shadow. The light is the appearance of Christ as a distinct, cosmic, sun-like Being in the Earth's ether. The shadow is the work of his adversaries.

This light of the New Age enables all to build a new vision of the Christ. This process began in the first part of the 20th century and is the product of the nascent but ever-growing activity of the Grail organ in the brain, already referred to. Through the practice of meditation, you learn to put the physical body asleep while keeping your thinking Ego wide-awake and alert. This power of overcoming sleep is the same power that develops the Grail chakra. You learn to shape it, and your thinking, into an ideal organic 'tool' with which you first gain a foothold in the supersensible, cosmic or etheric world. Subsequently you find your way on into the higher worlds. In this way, your thinking becomes a fully self-conscious, light-filled spiritual seeing, as your thoughts become feelings, and your feelings a magically informative and outwardly effective activity. This is the new mode of vision, the new state of being human, which has been spoken of and written about by many highly developed individuals in recent times, most clearly, scientifically and comprehensively by Steiner (1861 -1925).

Thus, we live in a time of a grand new Mystery. It is the task of Esoteric Christianity to both facilitate and spread this new knowledge, vision and understanding, which is in effect the building of a totally new body of Christ or church.

Through the practice of Esoteric Christianity, you develop a light in your thinking which shines out of you and into the formative life-sphere of the etheric world where, for you, it illuminates the figure of Christ with which your own light unites. More and more people will acquire this faculty over the next hundreds and thousands of years, but a beginning can be made right now by anyone who possesses an open, peace-loving heart.

#0003 - 031018 - C0 - 203/127/6 - PB - 9780954025588